In November of 2009, as this book was going to print, a securities fraud case discussed in Chapters 2 and 7 against two former Bear Stearns hedge fund managers, Ralph Cioffi and Matthew Tannin, was decided. The jury acquitted both defendants in the criminal case alleging conspiracy, fraud, and other charges, brought by the Justice Department in federal court in Brooklyn, New York. A Securities and Exchange Commission civil complaint remained outstanding at the time.

HEDGE FUNDS HUMBLED

The Seven Mistakes That Brought Hedge Funds to Their Knees and How They Will Rise Again

Trevor Ganshaw

McGraw Hill

New York   Chicago   San Francisco   Lisbon   London   Madrid   Mexico City
Milan   New Delhi   San Juan   Seoul   Singapore   Sydney   Toronto

1 2 3 4 5 6 7 8 9 0 DOC/DOC 0 1 5 4 3 2 1 0 9

ISBN 978-0-07-163712-1
MHID 0-07-163712-5

This publication is designed to provide accurate and authoritative information in regard to the subject matter covered. It is sold with the understanding that neither the author nor the publisher is engaged in rendering legal, accounting, futures/securities trading, or other professional service. If legal advice or other expert assistance is required, the services of a competent professional person should be sought.

—*From a Declaration of Principles jointly adopted by a Committee of the American Bar Association and a Committee of Publishers*

McGraw-Hill books are available at special quantity discounts to use as premiums and sales promotions, or for use in corporate training programs. To contact a representative, please e-mail us at bulksales@mcgraw-hill.com.

This book is printed on acid-free paper.

To Kaitlin, Sara, and Eric

CONTENTS

Introduction

THE TALE OF A SHARK

Eight million dollars. Even by the rarified standards of the contemporary art scene, it was a staggering number, one of the largest price tags ever affixed to an artist's work.

The work was a 14-foot tiger shark, pickled in a tank of formaldehyde. Steven A. Cohen, the billionaire founder of the hedge fund SAC Capital, was the buyer. As it turned out, the shark had not been properly preserved, and it was actually decomposing from the inside out. A problem? Not in the world of hedge fund masters. A special team was dispatched to capture and embalm a new shark that would be swapped for the original wrinkled, rotting carcass. The expense of the replacement, according to Cohen, was "inconsequential."

Oddly enough, the shark served as an apt metaphor for the hedge fund industry as it was at the time: awe inspiring, reveling in excess, and, in some ways, slowly rotting from the inside out.

With its promise of vast riches, everyone wanted a piece of the action. The number of hedge funds grew from a few hundred in the early 1990s to more than 9,000 in the United States alone by 2007. Assets skyrocketed, reaching $2.9 trillion in Q2 2008—up an astonishing $2.0 trillion since 2003.

Not satisfied with just a few trillion, the industry leveraged this capital by two to three times or more, enough to make long and short investments that approached a total of $10 trillion and generated annual fees of more than $100 billion for the anointed few.

And then, in 2008, it all came crashing down.

Rattled by the Lehman Brothers bankruptcy that September, banks began to yank financing from excessively leveraged hedge funds. Equally nervous investors, panicked by the growing market uncertainty, also rushed to redeem their capital. Stuck in overcrowded, thinly traded investments and armed with few options, many hedge funds were forced to dump assets into an increasingly unforgiving black hole of market illiquidity.

For some, this perfect storm ended in collapse, a complete wipeout of investor capital. In most cases, performance simply fell off a cliff; the industry went on to record its worst performance ever, down 20% for the year. More than 1,400 hedge funds, 14% of the industry, closed shop in 2008.[1]

Investors requested to redeem an estimated $1 trillion in hedge fund investments but managed to grab back only a fraction of that amount as the hedge funds tried to block the exodus of capital through "gates" and withdrawal suspensions.

Once the tide was out, some of the most stunning frauds in history were revealed, including the legendary Bernie Madoff, in his invisible $65 billion swimming trunks, and scam artist Samuel Israel, who scrawled a faked farewell to the world—"suicide is painless"—on the hood of his car.

Hedge funds have been *humbled*, and if the $8 million dead shark is any indication, the industry needed some humbling.

This book explores the seven key flaws that led to the industry's violent downfall in 2008: uncontrolled leverage, inadequate risk management, flawed fee structures, overcrowded strategies, the "Peter Principle" problem of too much capital, capital instability, and the lax controls that enabled fraud.

Fortunately, there is a bright side to this tale: what hasn't killed the industry will ultimately make it stronger. The thinning of the hedge fund herd will create more attractive investment opportunities that will produce better risk-adjusted returns. Risk management and fund governance will improve. Investors will demand better and more balanced fee structures. All of these factors, over the long term, will create a better and more sustainable product for both managers and investors. As all good hedge fund managers know, greed is good. Humility, it seems, may now be an essential part of keeping it that way.

The Beginning

It may surprise some readers to learn that the seeds of this madness were planted quite recently, around 2000. At about this time, the true "institutionalization" of the industry began.

As pension plans, university endowments, and other institutional investors began to diversify away from their traditional fixed income and equity investment strategies, they sought investments that would generate attractive, stable returns while exhibiting low correlation to the bond and equity markets. To these ends, investors dramatically increased their allocations to a variety of alternative investments that included hedge funds, private equity, real estate, and others.

Hedge fund managers, being the enterprising group they are, were not about to be left out of this multitrillion-dollar bonanza. But their industry had to adapt to meet the institutional investor's objectives.

In the 1990s, the hedge fund industry comprised a few hundred funds that focused largely on two strategies—global macro and long-short equity—and managed a total of less than $500 billion.

For the most part, these smaller funds did not meet the high standards that institutional investors were looking for. These investors were not about to entrust hundreds of billions to entities that were more like garage bands than Goldman Sachs. They wanted larger, multibillion-dollar "institutionalized" funds with fully built-out legal, compliance, operations, accounting, and finance teams to support the fund's investment operations. They also wanted a more diversified set of strategies that produced uncorrelated, stable, double-digit returns.

As it turned out, the industry was more than happy to super-size. Over the next decade, assets under management (AUM) became increasingly concentrated in the hands of a few hundred multibillion-dollar managers. By 2008, 80% of all assets were controlled by just 390 funds, each managing more than $1 billion.[2]

Additionally, as Figure I-1 highlights, hedge funds began to diversify away from long-short and global macro strategies as they sought to provide more investment opportunities that fit the low volatility, low correlation objectives of their investors.

Apparently, the growth program worked. As the industry evolved, it continued to provide consistent, attractive returns, drawing institutions back to hedge funds again and again with more aggressive allocations. Between 2006 and 2007 alone, hedge funds took in

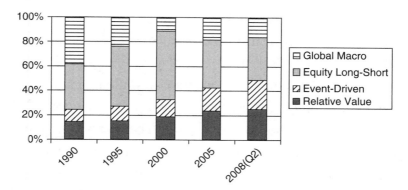

Figure I-1 Hedge fund breakdown by strategy
Source: AIMA's Roadmap to Hedge Funds, November 2008

more than $1 trillion. At the peak in early 2008, hedge fund AUM had grown by approximately $2 trillion in less than five years!

With this capital, however, came a new, unofficial set of rules. If a hedge fund could not reach a critical mass of at least $1 billion in AUM, it was unlikely to get a seat at the table. Few institutional investors wanted to represent more than 10% of a fund's assets, limiting the size of allocations to smaller funds. Second, in an

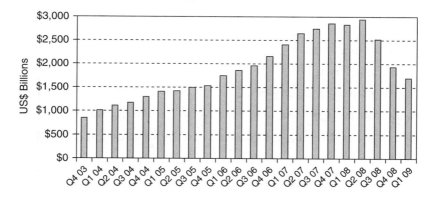

Figure I-2 Hedge fund asset growth, 2003 to 2009
Source: HFN Hedge Fund Industry Asset Flow/Performance Report, March 31, 2009

attempt to place their capital in safe hands, institutions wanted to invest in large, established funds with substantial infrastructure and a track record of successful investing.

Once a fund reached this critical mass (while maintaining reasonable investment returns), it could join the multibillion-dollar club and swim in the flood of capital that was pouring into the industry. Membership in this rarified circle entitled top *individual* hedge fund managers to more than $2 billion in personal earnings in 2007. Even second tier managers took home more than $100 million in a single year. Below that billion-dollar ceiling, the lack of capital limited access to fees, which restricted a fund's ability to attract top talent. It also made big investments in risk management systems, compliance teams, and other key elements of infrastructure potentially unfeasible.

While thousands of hedge funds chased trillions of dollars, there were almost *no* official rules to govern the game. There was effectively no outside regulation; access to leverage was virtually unlimited; few transparency requirements existed; and accounting standards were unprepared for the scope and complexity of risk being assumed in the industry.

As you might guess, this kind of Wild West environment produced a number of hedge fund managers who were willing to bet big at the casino, which led to an array of high profile winners and spectacular, multibillion-dollar disasters. Chronicled in the following chapters are many of the biggest blowups, including Amaranth Advisors (−65%), Bear Stearns hedge funds (−100%), Sowood Capital Management (−56%), and others.

All of this might well bring investors to ask some basic questions. How could multibillion-dollar hedge funds, which held capital preservation as a top priority, suddenly evaporate in a few days? What were the key factors that led to catastrophic failure in these funds? How did the funds' risk management teams overlook the strategic flaws? We will explore all of these questions in the chapters that follow.

Some Background

For readers less familiar with the hedge fund industry, the following few pages will provide a brief history, outline its most actively pursued strategies, and describe the counterparties that support the funds. For those already familiar with these topics, feel free to skip ahead to Chapter 1.

According to industry lore, the first hedge fund was launched around 1950 by Alfred Winslow Jones. He operated a long-short equity fund, utilized modest leverage, and created attractive double-digit returns. Jones's success inspired many others to follow in his footsteps, and for the next 50 years, the strategies underlying most hedge funds remained largely focused on either long-short equity or global macro. Not until the turn of the century did institutionalization spur the evolution of a more diverse set of relative value and event-driven funds.

Contrary to popular belief, no hedge fund actually "hedges" all of its risks. If it did so, there would be no returns. Instead, each fund tries to create hedges that (1) provide some protection in certain downside scenarios and (2) increase the probability of winning by creating option like payoff profiles in which it wins big under one set of outcomes and loses significantly less in others.

Hedge Fund Strategies

A few of the more common types of hedge fund strategies include long-short equity, global macro, relative value, and event-driven.

Long-Short Equity

As the name suggests, funds pursuing this strategy invest in long equity positions hedged with short sales of stocks or stock indexes. Some funds use fundamental research to target growth or value stocks; others are focused on specific sectors or emerging markets. For the most part, the assets underlying these funds are actively traded. In general, this liquidity allows them to accommodate shorter investor lockups.

Global Macro

Funds pursuing a global macro strategy generally take positions in a broad array of financial instruments, including sovereign debt securities, currencies, commodities, rate sensitive instruments, and a host of derivative securities. Through these positions, the funds seek to capture value from anticipated trends or moments in the global macroeconomic environment. In most cases, these trends tend to be driven by changes in government policies, economic growth or instability, capital flows, fiscal instability, or other systemic country- or region-specific issues.

Relative Value

Relative value strategies target and exploit differences in the relative economic attractiveness of one security versus another. These differences tend to be measured by comparing the expected return of an investment for a given set of risks, such as subordination, maturity, liquidity, covenant features, asset coverage, etc. Managers then express these value differences through positions that are long investments in the relatively cheap securities and short the relatively rich.

Most funds that pursue this strategy seek these opportunities within corporate capital structures. Capital structure arbitrage, for example, is generally focused on relative value opportunities within a single corporate capital structure. Fixed income arbitrage, on the other hand, tends to seek opportunities in the debt or fixed income derivative securities of different corporate or sovereign issuers. Convertible bond arbitrage and volatility arbitrage are other examples within the relative value category. Because credit instruments play such a large role in many relative value strategies, the underlying assets can be significantly less liquid and more difficult to trade in times of stress.

Event-Driven

Event-driven funds seek to exploit pricing inefficiencies created by actual or anticipated corporate events such as mergers or acquisitions, spin-offs or split-offs of certain businesses, defaults, bankruptcies or other distress events, recapitalizations, and other reorganization events. Funds within this category include merger or risk arbitrage funds (which seek to capture the difference between the offered purchase price and the current market price of a stock that is subject to a takeover or merger offer), distressed debt funds, and activist funds (which make concentrated investments in companies where they believe they can push for changes that will boost the value of its shares).

Counterparties

Counterparties such as prime brokerage firms, banks, administrators, and auditors also play a key role in the success of most hedge funds.

Prime Brokerage Firms

Prime brokerage firms provide a variety of services that are essential to the operation of a hedge fund:

- Financing (leverage) for certain assets

- Securities lending for short sale activity

- Global custody (which includes holding and/or safeguarding physical securities and clearing services)

For most prime brokers (PBs), the financing they provide is generally limited to a select group of liquid, actively traded securities such as common stock, corporate bonds, convertible debt, and listed options. A hedge fund must seek financing elsewhere for other less-liquid securities like bank loans; structured securities such as collateralized debt obligations (CDOs); and other derivative securities.

Because access to capital is the primary component of a prime broker's service, most PBs are embedded in major banks or securities firms. Since they carry significant capital at risk on a daily basis, PBs will also perform detailed due diligence on a fund both initially and on an ongoing basis. As a result, a strong set of PB relationships can lend significant credibility to a fund.

Prime brokers do not typically provide P&L reporting, yearly auditing, or security pricing and valuation. Leading prime brokers include Goldman Sachs, Morgan Stanley, Deutsche Bank, UBS, Bank of America/Merrill Lynch, and J.P. Morgan.

Banks

The primary role of a bank in the hedge fund industry is to provide financing for the assets that prime brokers will not leverage. Some of the assets included in this group are bank loans, over-the-counter derivatives, structured securities like CDOs, and other complex or less actively traded securities.

Most hedge funds also like to keep at least 15% to 20% of their AUM in unencumbered cash at a bank separate from their prime brokers. This ensures liquidity for the fund in times of market stress or a default at the prime broker.

Hedge Fund Administrators

A strong fund administrator is at the core of any well-run hedge fund, providing several key services:

- Preparation and maintenance of full accounting records for a fund
- Portfolio pricing using independent, recognized pricing sources
- Calculation of fees and accruals
- Calculation of net asset value and preparation of client statements
- Preparation of weekly and/or monthly financial statements in conformity with generally accepted accounting principles (GAAP)

Arguably, if all of these functions are performed well by an established firm, the risk of inaccurate financial statements or fraud is minimized. Some hedge funds still "self-administrate"; for these funds, the risk of misstatements or fraud can be considerably higher.

Audit Firms

The role of the auditor is also indispensable to accurate financial accounting. The fund's auditor will thoroughly review all of the financial statements on an annual basis to determine if they conform to GAAP. This review requires not only diligence on the auditor's part but also coordination with the employees and administrator of a fund; when executed well, it is an excellent means of confirming the legitimacy of a fund's activities. It is, however, critical that a fund engage a nationally recognized audit firm to perform this service. Small, poorly staffed, and even sham audit firms have been at the center of a number of frauds.

one

THE TRUE EVIL IN HEDGE FUND COMPENSATION

(NO, IT'S NOT GREED)

For the past several years, *Alpha* magazine has provided an annual ranking of the top earners in the hedge fund industry. Each year, the numbers at the top of the heap grew more astonishing. By 2007, the top 25 individuals had earned a combined $20 billion — including five managers who made more than $1.5 billion *each* in a single year. Even the list's bottom feeders walked away with more than $200 million apiece. Many entrepreneurs in other industries have attained such wealth, but there are few outside the hedge fund industry who became so rich so quickly.

Predictably, the recipients of this bonanza were not afraid to spend their newfound wealth. Reports of the inevitable excess proliferated: private jets, mansions, longer-than-yours yachts, weddings at Versailles, $8 million pickled sharks, and so on. Even the horrendous investment performance of 2008 turned out to be

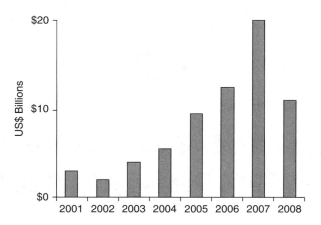

Figure 1-1 Combined income of the top 25 hedge fund managers in billions
Source: Institutional Investor's *Alpha* magazine

nothing more than a speed bump to the hedge fund Brinks truck; nine- and ten-figure paychecks continued to be cut.

With the world mired in a deep recession in 2009, it was hardly surprising that accusations of greed were being thrown about daily by national leaders, editorial boards, talk show hosts—anyone, really, looking to score easy points. President Obama called Wall Street bonuses "shameful" within his first hundred days. French president Nicolas Sarkozy declared that he was "shocked" by the "system of bonuses for traders." "That's what we need to change," he said.

Terrific sound bites, perhaps, but the true evil of hedge fund bonuses has less to do with greed than with the inherent flaws embedded in many compensation schemes—flaws that can encourage excessive risk taking and promote an array of other unintended incentives.

To begin with, any investor seeking to place capital with a hedge fund must agree to the predetermined fee structure. This typically includes the management fee, which is paid quarterly and derived

Table 1-1 Top Hedge Fund Earners

Person	Fund	Earnings, Millions
2007		
John Paulson	Paulson & Company	$3,700
George Soros	Soros Fund Management	$2,900
James Simons	Renaissance Technologies	$2,800
Philip Falcone	Harbinger Capital Partners	$1,700
Kenneth Griffin	Citadel Investment Group	$1,500
Steven Cohen	SAC Capital Advisors	$900
Timothy Barakett	Atticus Capital	$750
Stephen Mandel, Jr.	Lone Pine Capital	$710
John Griffin	Blue Ridge Capital	$625
O. Andreas Halvorsen	Viking Global Investors	$520
2008		
James Simons	Renaissance Technologies	$2,500
John Paulson	Paulson & Company	$2,000
John Arnold	Centaurus Energy	$1,500
George Soros	Soros Fund Management	$1,100
Raymond Dalio	Bridgewater Associates, Inc.	$780
Bruce Kovner	Caxton Associates LLC	$640
David Shaw	D.E. Shaw & Co.	$275
Stanley Druckenmiller	Duquesne Capital Mgmt.	$260
David Hardling	Brevan Howard Asset Mgmt.	$250
Alan Howard	Blue Ridge Capital	$250

Source: Institutional Investor magazine

from the amount of assets managed. It also includes an annual performance fee that gives the manager a percentage of any gains that are produced and, in many cases, an expense pass-through on certain costs the fund incurs. Although the levels most frequently cited for the industry involve a 2% management fee and a 20% performance fee, there are countless variations ranging from 1% and 10% to 3% and 30%. The particular structure a manager chooses is derived from the strength of the fund's track record, the investor lockup period, performance hurdles, and so on.

Given these percentages and the amounts of money being handled, it's quite simple to determine how such enormous compensation levels are reached. If a hedge fund with a 2% and 20% fee structure is managing assets totaling $5 billion, gross fees of $300 million can be generated by the good (but not spectacular!) return of 20% in a year (2% management fee plus a 4% performance fee).

The issue at hand is not one of "fairness." These fees are the simple, direct result of a contract entered into by a group of experienced investors and a manager. Everyone reads the fine print and signs; if a manager then delivers on the agreement and generates positive performance, she has earned her compensation, however high it may be.

Rather than bemoaning greed, it's far more productive to determine if hedge fund compensation formulas create proper manager incentives. That is, do they foster alignment between the manager's interests and the risk-return objectives of the investors? Or do they instead create adverse incentives that divert a fund from its longer-term investment objectives and lead to increased risk or even catastrophic loss?

A Free Call Option

One aspect of hedge fund compensation that seems to invite excessive risk is the inherent asymmetry of the compensation formula. By design, these formulas create a "call option" payoff with a huge upside for good returns and a very restricted downside for poor ones. For instance, if a hedge fund is particularly successful, gaining 20% to 40% in a year, the payoff can be enormous, totaling 4% to 8% of AUM in incentive fees on top of a 2% management fee. If the hedge fund loses the same amount in a year, the fund still receives its 2% management fee but no incentive fee. Despite this optionality, it has been very rare for a fund to allow fee "clawbacks" — the return of fees from a prior year if the current year is substantially down, even if the underlying assets are the same or similar. So not only is the fee structure a win–win for hedge funds in any given year, it is a win–win from year to year.

The only downside for the manager is the existence of a "high water mark" (HWM) in many funds. An HWM is a stipulation that requires the manager to make back any previous year's losses before new future performance fees can be paid. For small losses, this can be an effective mechanism for aligning a manager's interests with those of the fund's investors, but in the event of large losses — such as those accrued throughout the industry in 2008 — the HWM is problematic. The managers, unlikely to recoup the HWM in the near term, face the prospect of several years without performance fees. This in turn makes the attraction and retention of top talent much more challenging, which further reduces the likelihood of attractive future returns.

A small number of funds have attempted to mitigate these difficulties by creating modified HWMs that allow for a reduced performance fee, typically 10%, to be paid after posting a down year, with the provision that this lower fee will remain in effect until some greater percentage (often 130%) of the losses are recovered. This kind of fee structure helps to minimize the problems of talent retention and operation. However, for any fund facing deep performance losses without such a modification to its fee structure, the HWM can prove to be a death knell, forcing the manager to close the fund and attempt to start a new one. Given the high cost of asset liquidation, closing a fund is no picnic for either the fund or the investors.

However you slice it, though, each of these provisions helps to ensure that the hedge fund manager always shares in the upside while the investor always eats the downside.

Fool Me Twice?

Some argue that the counterbalance to asymmetric hedge fund economics is the loss of a manager's reputation after a fund has failed. According to this argument, a poorly performing or failed fund will so damage the manager's most valuable asset—his reputation—as to end his career in the industry. Thus, the manager's innate desire to remain in the club of unimaginable wealth will always curb any urge he may have to exploit the advantages of the imbedded call option.

It's a nice argument, and it would be nicer if it were true, but the recent success of failed hedge fund managers blows this argument full of holes. In fact, managers have jumped clear of some of the biggest flameouts on record and into new positions where they quickly attracted new capital. John Meriwether's fund, Long-Term Capital Management, infamously collapsed in 1998. The next year, he launched JWM Partners LLC, which flaunted close to $2 billion in AUM by early 2008[1]; Geoff Grant, cofounder and CIO of Peloton Partners, launched a new fund, Grant Capital Partners, only months after his former $2 billion firm collapsed under the weight of steep losses and lost financing[2]. Nick Maounis, founder of Amaranth Advisors LLC, who oversaw the largest hedge fund collapse in history, also has a new venture in the works. The list goes on and on.

In the end, the call option embedded in the hedge fund fee structure results in unfathomable riches for the manager if things go well and "getting by" on management fees if they don't. In a worst-case scenario, if the fund fails altogether, the manager can simply close it and reboot with a new fund.

The dangers of this asymmetry are pretty clear. In an effort to maximize the value of the call option, a fund might take on excessive leverage, engage in high position concentration (that is, bet the ranch), adopt inadequately hedged positions, or take other big risks.

Unfortunately, the incentives created by the compensation call option are not limited to senior managers. The same type of asymmetric payout exists for the portfolio managers of most funds as well. Many funds separate portfolio managers into separate strategies, or "silos," and give them a percentage of the upside in their investments for the year, typically equaling 50% to 75% of the fund's ~20% performance fee, or 10% to 15% of their profits.

Smarter funds also incorporate some portion of overall fund performance into portfolio manager compensation formulas as a way to better align trader incentives and mitigate the temptation to bet big in any one portfolio. Even with these modifications, though, most portfolio manager pay models remain entrenched in a call option mentality: big gains generate big compensation, while losses net you a salary and one or more chances to shoot for the moon again.

At most hedge funds, a risk management team exists that is tasked with monitoring portfolio manager attempts to take outsized risks. Unfortunately, the track record of these efforts within the industry has been at best inconsistent. Consider the case of Brian Hunter of Amaranth Advisors. In 2005, he made a big, bullish bet on natural gas that paid off handsomely when Hurricane Rita hit the United States. His pay for the year was estimated to be approximately $75 million. Fresh off this stunning success, he ramped up his risk in the natural gas market, amassing more than $10 billion in trades and controlling an amount equal to, at one point, roughly 25% of the annual U.S. residential natural gas consumption. This time, however, his luck wasn't as good. Less than one year after his $75 million payday, his trades contributed to losses of more than $6 billion and led to the collapse of the firm. Today, he is gainfully employed at a new fund and apparently still enjoying what is left of his $75 million from Amaranth. (See Chapter 5 for a more detailed discussion of Amaranth and Brian Hunter.)

Recognizing the flaws in this compensation strategy, some funds have developed nonformulaic, subjective "anti-silo" pay plans that incorporate individual portfolio manager P&L, overall firm performance, movement of capital from underperforming sectors or strategies, information sharing, etc. While these pay plans do address many of the problems associated with the fee call option, they can also drive exceptionally talented managers to seek potentially bigger payoffs at funds with formulaic compensation.

Perhaps the best defense against imbalances and abuses will always be greater ownership of the downside risk by a fund's partners. The best risk management teams tend to be found at firms where partners have the majority of their own wealth invested in the funds, such as Steve Cohen at SAC Capital and Jim Simons at Renaissance Capital. Loss of reputation is one thing. Loss of one's fortune is quite another.

Realized Fees on Unrealized Gains

For many hedge funds, paying fees on investment gains produced by the fund is a relatively fair and simple matter. If the fund's underlying investments are actively traded—as is the case with many long-short equity, global macro, and commodity funds—then the fund can easily respond to any loss of its equity or debt capital by quickly selling (or buying, if short) assets at prevailing market prices and returning the capital. In these cases, investors exit the fund having paid fees that accurately reflect the fund's performance from initial allocation to redemption.

Other funds, however—particularly those that invest in long-dated and less liquid assets—can sometimes create a much less balanced and more painful fee outcome for investors. In these cases, many funds will finance these longer-dated assets with monthly or quarterly equity and debt capital. If this capital is lost or redeemed, as it was for many funds in 2008, the fund can be forced to sell its illiquid assets at heavily discounted or fire sale prices. For an investor who has paid 20% performance fees year after year, a premature sale of these investments at deeply discounted prices can wipe out years of gains and leave the investor stuck with fees paid on gains that were never realized.

Table 1-2 The Toll of Hedge Fund Fees

	Capital Balance	Gross Investment Return, 15%	Management Fees, 2%	Performance Fees, 20%	Net Return
Starting	$1,000,000				
Year 1	$1,104,000	$150,000	$20,000	$26,000	$104,000
Year 2	$1,218,816	$165,600	$22,080	$28,704	$114,816
Year 3	$1,345,573	$182,822	$24,376	$31,689	$126,757
Totals			$66,456	$86,393	$345,573
(25% Loss)	$1,009,180	−$336,393	$0	$0	$9,180
3-Year Totals			$66,456	$86,393	$9,180
Percent of Beginning Investment			6.6%	8.6%	0.9%

Consider the hypothetical $1 million hedge fund investment shown in Table 1-2. This simplified analysis assumes that a hedge fund generated 15% gross returns per year for three years and received a 2% management fee and 20% performance fee each year. Assume that on the first day of the fourth year, the fund lost a substantial part of its debt and equity capital and recorded a 25% decline due to forced sales of illiquid assets (effectively, this is what happened to scores of funds in 2008). At the end of year three, the $1 million investment had generated a net compounded return of 34.5% after management fees of $66,456 and performance fees of $86,393. Not bad. However, the 25% loss early the next year is a killer. The fund's three-year annualized return drops to 0.9%, and yet the fund retains performance fees equal to 8.6% of the initial investment for performance that was never realized. Total fees for the three years exceeded 15%.

Prior to the credit crisis, very few hedge funds that trafficked in illiquid securities had a mechanism to deal with this problem.

After 2008, however, many investors, having been flogged by fees on unrealized gains, called for the use of clawback mechanisms in funds that invest in longer-dated assets. Clawbacks are a means to better match performance fees with the realization of the performance. They allow investors to recover all or a portion of previously paid performance fees after a period of negative performance. CalPERS (California Public Employees' Retirement System), a California public pension fund and one of the largest hedge fund investors, and the Utah Retirement Systems (URS) both endorsed this approach in 2009.

In practice, however, it is difficult to implement clawbacks. After all, a future promise to return fees is only as good as the creditworthiness of the obligor. Also, if a fund collapses, there may be little left to return. One option that has gained backing from institutional investors involves escrowing a portion of annual performance fees in a segregated account for a term of several years. For other managers of illiquid assets, such as private equity funds, deferred performance fees are commonplace: a private equity "carried interest" performance fee is paid only when the investment is realized and investors have received repayment of their original capital. As the hedge fund industry looks forward, a clawback feature will most likely be part of many successful funds.

Artificial Alpha

A related but far less common problem with hedge fund fees involves, for lack of a better term, "artificial" alpha. The term *alpha* describes a manager's ability to generate returns in excess of a benchmark index or riskless interest rate. For the vast majority of managers, this alpha is achieved through deep fundamental research, superior market or industry knowledge, and strong trading skills, among other advantages.

In some cases, however, managers can either knowingly or unwittingly generate excess returns that appear to be real due to their size and consistency but are actually short-term gains created by leveraging small interest payments or other consistently paid premiums in exchange for taking on large downside exposures. Like many other dubious investment propositions, it works brilliantly—until the hurricane blows in. Only then is the fallacy of the venture uncovered.

An appropriate analogy for this type of strategy is a portfolio of short put options. For example, consider a hypothetical strategy of selling put options on the S&P 500 (not a specific strategy that hedge funds employ but illustratively similar to others that are utilized). For a given dollar amount of capital, you could generate annual premiums equaling approximately 10% to 15% a year by selling 15% out-of-the-money S&P put options. In exchange for this premium, you would be required to assume all of the downside risk in the index below a decline of 15% for the year. The probability that these put options will be exercised is somewhere between 20% and 25%. If the options are not exercised (a 75% to 80% probability), then the manager will generate annual gross returns of 10% to 15%. If leverage is used, the returns would easily exceed 20%.

In a bull market, this strategy could successfully generate this type of return for years. When the inevitable fall arrives, however, any decline in the index greater than 15% is fully borne by the investors in the fund, possibly leading to large losses. For hedge fund managers with a 2% and 20% fee structure, the lack of a claw-back feature makes this type of strategy very attractive: they enjoy both the 2% management fee and 20% performance fees on returns of 10% to 15% or more for years. When the market tanks, they are under no obligation to return their previously earned performance fees.

Selling Subprime Puts

Granted, this S&P put option example is almost silly in its simplicity. Nonetheless, it is remarkably analogous to the return profile some hedge funds pursued in the boom years. And, as with our put option example, when the music stopped, the outcome for investors in those funds was no laughing matter.

One example of artificial alpha involved the Bear Stearns hedge fund. The main strategy of Bear's hedge fund was to invest in structured bonds backed by subprime mortgages, which support the least creditworthy homeowners and therefore tend to suffer significantly greater losses than higher-quality mortgages during recessions or other times of economic pain. The Bear fund was a heavy buyer of these bonds, which paid less than 2% over the base interest rate. To amplify this small spread and create net returns of 10% to 12% after fees, the fund leveraged its assets by somewhere in the vicinity of ten times the amount of investor capital.

For years, while the housing bubble continued to expand, this strategy earned consistently strong returns, attracted more investor capital, and generated a mountain of fees for the fund's managers. Then, in late 2007, home prices began to fall, many adjustable-rate mortgages began to reset higher, and the default rates on subprime mortgages began to skyrocket. Under the weight of huge invest-ment losses, high leverage, illiquid assets, and ineffective hedges, the fund collapsed, resulting in a near-total loss to shareholders.

Although it was hard to see at the time, owning exposure to sub-prime mortgages was almost identical to being short put options. The manager received modest but dependable quarterly interest payments in exchange for bearing all of the downside risk of sub-prime mortgage defaults. When the subprime market collapsed, so did the fund. (See Chapter 2 for a more detailed look at the Bear Stearns fund.)

In general, cases of artificial alpha are relatively rare. When they do occur, overpayment of fees for unrealized gains are just the beginning of an investor's nightmare—yet another reason clawbacks are an important feature for investors.

As you can tell from this discussion, hedge fund compensation plans are bull market structures, designed with the expectation that funds would never lose money. For years the hedgehogs were right. However, now that the tide has gone out and the flaws have been exposed, pay plans will need to be altered to draw capital back into the industry. Funds must find a way to create fee struc-tures that correspond to the duration and liquidity of their underlying investments.

For managers of liquid, easily tradable assets, fee holdback fea-tures are arguably less useful. In these cases, it may be more important to achieve better incentive alignment through increased ownership in the fund. In particular, investors should seek to invest with managers who have a substantial amount of their own net worth in their funds. Investors may also want to consider a provision that requires managers to further invest a portion of annual performance fees in the fund to create additional ownership and better alignment of incentives.

For managers investing in longer-dated and possibly less liquid assets, a mechanism to hold or claw back performance fees is more important. In these cases, funds should be subject to a clawback on performance fees over a period of time that matches the duration of the underling assets in a stressed environment. For many credit managers, this is probably a period of at least two to three years.

Looking forward, hedge fund fee structures should seek to encourage greater manager downside ownership and restrict performance fee payment to performance realization. Those which satisfy these objectives will foster better alignment of manager and investor interests and create greater long-term value for both.

two

EXCESSIVE LEVERAGE
GORGING AT THE BUFFET

If failed hedge funds had a black box—surveillance tapes to pull from the wreckage—many would reveal a history of excessive use of leverage coupled with an almost reckless disregard for its potential downside. During the boom years, calm markets and easy access to capital caused many hedge funds to become increasingly complacent with higher levels of risk. And of all the risks they were willing to assume, excessive leverage was by far the most prevalent, easiest to obtain, cheapest to carry, and, without question, laden with the greatest threats to both the performance and survival of many funds. Name almost any disaster from recent memory: Amaranth, Sowood, Peloton, Bear Stearns, even Long-Term Capital Management's collapse back in the late 1990s. Every one of them carried excessive leverage that contributed greatly to its downfall.

The allure and danger of using leverage are both pretty obvious. With each dollar of equity capital a fund manager receives from investors, there is the potential to borrow additional capital from banks and prime brokerage firms. If the cost of this debt is less than the expected return on the underlying investments—which is exactly what any self-confident manager expects—the leverage will enhance the excess positive returns. If, however, the strategy unexpectedly loses money, the leverage will magnify the loss.

In the midst of a tremendous, multiyear upward run, it is no surprise that virtually every fee-maximizing fund manager was willing to meet this bet—with serious money. Fortunately for them, there was no shortage of lenders willing to provide leverage. Before the 2008 credit crisis, banks and prime brokerage firms were eager to lend heavily to almost any hedge fund. The competition for market share by prime brokers ensured that leverage was abundant, exceptionally cheap, and available even to the most marginal players.

With so much leverage available, however, and with so many funds chasing similar assets, the price of many commonly targeted hedge fund investments shot up, lowering the expected returns. This, in turn, required any other hedge fund seeking competitive returns to lever-up as well; debt became almost a necessary component of any hedge fund strategy.

Even as overall leverage in the industry rose, there continued to be wide variation in the amount of leverage utilized by individual funds. Hedge funds with strategies that were perceived to be more volatile—such as equity long-short, equity event-driven, and commodity funds—tended to take a more conservative approach to leverage. Those that focused on ostensibly lower volatility assets—credit arbitrage, convertible arbitrage, and multi-strategy funds—utilized significantly more.

Before the credit crisis, long-short funds, according to prime brokerage data, typically invested in long positions that totaled 1.5 to 2 times their equity capital (i.e., they were 1.5 to 2 times leveraged). By contrast, multi-strategy, convertible, and other credit funds typically leveraged their portfolios at a higher level, usually at least 2 to 4 times. But some funds used much more than that—sometimes as much as 10 times the amount of their equity. At that level, the danger is clear: with 10 times the leverage, if investments managed by a hedge fund decline by 10% or more, the investors are wiped out.

This simple multiplier effect of leverage was just one strand in a spider web of risk that ensnared many funds and led to outsized losses in 2008. Investment losses, already magnified by excessive leverage, were often made significantly worse by the abrupt loss of debt financing, equity redemptions, and deeply illiquid investments, which sometimes forced the sale of assets at discounted or even fire sale prices.

Most hedge fund financing, for example, is short-term debt that must be "rolled"—renewed—periodically, often on a daily basis. When good times are on, this is no problem; capital rolls along effortlessly. But in times of stress, when the stability of a fund's capital structure is of greatest importance, banks are more likely to pull this debt, forcing a potentially untimely sale of fund assets. Similar laws of cause and effect govern the equity capital of hedge funds. With most funds carrying a three-month lockup on their equity capital, a few months of down performance in a hedge fund can quickly generate equity redemption requests that inevitably lead to additional asset sales. Furthermore, when capital instability in the hedge fund industry is widespread—and it certainly was in 2008—most hedge funds have to sell assets, but few have the capacity to buy, which makes market liquidity much more difficult to find for many common hedge fund investments. This raises the possibility of forced asset sales at unattractive prices, which can create more losses, which makes banks and equity investors even more jumpy, which can lead to more capital instability, and so on. This chapter explores all the stages of this downward spiral as well as some strategies hedge funds have used to avoid the grim circumstances posed by leverage, capital instability, and illiquidity.

Risk, Measured Many Ways

How does a hedge fund define leverage? Unfortunately, there is no straightforward answer. Generally, most will define leverage as the "gross long" positions divided by AUM. In the calculation of gross longs, all traditional debt and equity investments are included at market value and all swaps, futures, options, and other derivative contracts are valued at the full notional* risk exposure assumed through the contract. Using this calculation, if a hedge fund manager has $1 billion of investor capital under management, and the fund has total gross long positions of $3 billion, the fund is considered to be three times levered, utilizing $2 billion of total debt. A flaw in this formulation is that it ignores any short positions a hedge fund manager employs in the portfolio. Consequently, the actual leverage may be either overestimated or understated depending on the extent to which the short positions offset or significantly reduce the risk inherent in the longs.

A second approach is to tally the gross long *and* short positions and divide the sum of these two numbers by the AUM. This method not only ignores the potential of short positions to reduce risk, it

---

*The amount of exposure to the underlying asset assumed through the exercise of the contract.

actually penalizes them by including them in the leverage number. This approach makes more sense in long-short equity funds and other situations where long and short positions are not necessarily intended to provide direct offsetting risk reduction. It is not a good fit for multi-strategy, capital structure arbitrage, convertible, or other credit funds where short positions often provide direct risk offsets to the long positions. (For example, many of these funds utilize a number of highly correlated hedges such as position-specific credit default swaps—short positions that are effectively insurance policies against the default of a specific loan or bond in its portfolio.)

Finally, some managers look at net exposure (long positions minus short positions, divided by AUM) as a means of measuring leverage. This method completely overlooks the very real risk that the long and short positions may deviate significantly from the level of correlation they have historically experienced; in other words, they might not provide the expected (and necessary) offsetting hedge performance. Consequently, this approach tends to generally grossly understate leverage.

For the sake of simplicity, we will stick to the first of the aforementioned methods (gross long over AUM) as a simple measure of leverage.

Gorging at the Leverage Buffet

To sate the massive debt appetite of the hedge fund world, banks and prime brokerage firms laid out a long and well-stocked buffet of leverage. Like many buffet-style dining experiences, this one offered an exceptionally low-priced menu, vast quantities, and flavors for every appetite, keeping its hedge fund customers coming back to gorge themselves again and again.

Prime Brokerage Facilities

Prime brokerage financing was (and in all likelihood will continue to be) the largest source of hedge fund leverage, with an estimated total outstanding in 2008 of $2 trillion. The vast majority of this financing is structured with a very short fuse, providing hedge funds with certainty of financing for a period that ranges from just one day to a few months. Any financing committed for a period of one to three months or longer is typically provided on a "rolling" basis, which means that if the prime broker wants to change the terms of the financing, or pull it altogether, it provides notice and then, after a one- to three-month "term-out period," modifies the financing or terminates it. This financing is particularly well suited to very short duration strategies: long-short equity funds, risk arbitrage, equity event-driven strategies, and others. In the event of a termination, the fund simply sells shares (assuming the stocks they own are liquid), raises cash, and pays off the debt.

For high-yield bonds, convertible securities, and other credit instruments, things can get a little stickier. These securities tend to have longer lives (three to five years or longer) and a tendency, particularly in time of stress, to become significantly less liquid than equities. The risk is obvious: if the prime broker terminates or significantly raises the cost of a fund's financing, the fund could be forced to sell the investments into an illiquid or unattractive market. In a perfect world, the term of the debt would match the term of the investment, and many of these risks would be largely eliminated. Unfortunately for most hedge funds, longer-term financing is simply unavailable, making short-term prime broker financing the only game in town.

The cost of this financing? As with any other loan, it depends on the market environment. In the case of larger funds, before the credit crisis, the cost was typically around "50 bps through the middle." This meant that the fund would be charged a rate of fed funds, plus 25 bps (basis points) for net borrowings and would receive fed funds less 25 bps for net cash balances held. Sounds pretty cheap, doesn't it? So cheap that it was actually comparable to the borrowing levels at some of the biggest blue-chip corporations like IBM or GE. Not bad for a few dozen guys sitting in a leased office space.

For a prime broker, the real profit is not always derived from this type of thin margin lending; instead it tends to come from other key services including rehypothecation (lending of investor securities held by the broker) and security borrowing facilities (so managers can short sell stocks, bonds, and other securities).

In general, prime brokerage financing is available only for specific, actively traded hedge fund investments such as common stocks, high-yield and investment-grade bonds, convertible securities, traded options, and certain other derivative instruments. These facilities are generally not available for instruments such as bank loans, private investments, various collateralized loan obligations, asset-backed securities, and commodities.

Given the broad range of securities they finance and the ancillary services they provide, prime brokers are at the center of most hedge fund financing strategies.

Term Bank Debt

For other privately traded securities such as corporate bank loans and some other fixed income securities, hedge funds will generally seek to arrange for a separate term facility at a bank. These facilities are typically structured as "total return swaps," or TRSs. Here, the bank pays the total return of the bank loan (interest payments and price performance) to the hedge fund, and the hedge fund pays a modest fixed rate of interest. The amount of leverage provided to the hedge fund is equal to the difference between the market value of the loan and the amount of cash collateral (the "haircut") that the hedge fund posts against the swap. The bank holds the actual loan on its balance sheet as a hedge to its obligations under the TRS. The key benefit of a term TRS facility is that, at least during the boom years, it could provide for revolving use of a predetermined amount of leverage with a fixed set of terms for a much longer period of time than a prime brokerage facility—as much as one to three years.

Except for their longer duration, these facilities behave very similarly to prime brokerage financing. Each investment that goes into the term facility has a specified haircut assigned, which is based on a credit quality "grid" that determines the amount of leverage initially allocated to the investment. As prices for each security vary, cash margin is added or removed from the position to ensure daily maintenance of the original haircut levels. The major difference is that, at least theoretically, the lender cannot modify any terms, including the final maturity of the term bank facility, unless the fund violates certain covenants (a caveat examined later in this book).

Repos—The Land of Misfit Toys

For hedge funds, repurchase agreements—"repos"—are the financing vehicles that provide leverage for individual securities that cannot be financed through the traditional vendors, namely prime brokerage accounts or bank TRS facilities. Repos tend to accommodate a variety of more complex, structured securities, including tranches of collateralized loan or debt obligations (CLOs/CDOs), various types of residential or commercial mortgage-backed securities (RMBS/CMBS), asset-backed securities, and other less liquid (and less understood) "misfit" investments.

In this type of arrangement, the hedge fund manager sells a security to a bank with the understanding that the fund will repurchase it from the bank at a predetermined price on a certain date—usually between a day and a few months later. As a result, the manager maintains economic exposure to the asset but receives financing through the initial proceeds it receives from the "sale" of the asset. The bank, in turn, holds the asset as collateral against the fund's agreement to repurchase it. As with the other forms of hedge fund financing, there is an initial amount of leverage provided, and this level must be maintained if the market price of the asset varies. In this case, repo providers rely on a master repo agreement (MRA) to define the facilities' terms.

Overall, the repo market provides an attractive source of leverage for securities that are difficult to finance elsewhere. The level of leverage, however, that can be achieved through this form of financing is typically less aggressive than what is available for less complex securities in the prime brokerage market.

Medium-Term Notes and CLO Debt

Rounding out the leverage buffet are two other forms of longer-term hedge fund debt, both of which are difficult to establish except for the most seasoned managers at the largest firms.

Medium-term notes carry maturities up to five years and are typically issued into the public debt market by a subsidiary or holding company of the underlying investment vehicle. Citadel Finance Limited, a subsidiary of Citadel Investment Group, issued such a note in December 2006, reportedly raising $500 million[1] in a five-year structure. Historically, issuance of this type of debt has been quite limited; since the credit crisis began, it has been virtually nonexistent.

A second type of longer-term leverage that hedge funds utilized prior to the credit crisis was CLO (collateralized loan obligation) financing. CLO financing is a type of debt backed by a pool of corporate bank loan investments that act as collateral to secure the interest and principal payments on the debt sold. Under this strategy, more than 100 corporate bank loans are pooled, then a series of rated tranches of debt—with ratings ranging from AAA to BB—are sold against the pool of collateral. Historically, the rated tranches—AAA, AA, A, and BBB—were sold to institutional bond investors; they represented 85% to 90% of the value of the underlying loan collateral. As the creator of the CLO structure, the hedge fund put up all or some of the remaining capital in exchange for equity or subordinated debt securities. By owning the equity capital of the structure, the funds maintained both management responsibility for the underlying loan pool and the leveraged economics the structure generated.

From a risk-return perspective, this structure provided the highest security and lowest return to the AAA debt investors and vice versa for the equity. Mechanically, income from the underlying pool of loans trickles down, paying interest and principal to the highest rated tranches first and equity holders last. Losses from any defaulted loans bubble upward, hurting the hedge fund equity holders first and the debt investors only after lower tranches have been wiped out.

For a hedge fund, the amount of leverage and overall cost of financing it could achieve by establishing such a structure was astonishingly attractive. In the heyday of CLOs, 10 to 15 times leverage was commonplace at average rates as low as LIBOR (London Interbank Offered Rate) plus 35 to 45 bps. Once again, the hedge funds found a way to borrow billions of dollars at a few basis points wide of blue-chip corporate America.

Perhaps the most appealing feature of this debt was that it was nonrecourse to the hedge fund manager, meaning that the institutional investors that purchased the debt looked to only the underlying pool of bank loans that served as their collateral in the structure. If the manager of the CLO (the hedge fund) did not pay interest or principal when it was due, the debt investor's only recourse was to seize the bank loans in the CLO and had no claim to any other assets managed by the hedge fund.

For all their allure, these structures presented a few pitfalls to the funds as well. The first and perhaps most important consideration was that the structures required the manager to maintain a significant exposure to bank loans throughout the life of the vehicle. Therefore, unless the manager was able to sell the fund's equity interest in the vehicle, the fund had to hold a leveraged exposure to bank loans. For many years, this wasn't a problem. However, during the credit crisis, the price of bank loans plunged to about 60% of face, creating major losses in the leveraged equity that many hedge funds held in these structures.

The second problem was that CLOs typically carried a series of internal covenants that governed the quality of the bank debt held in the pool. If enough underlying loans either defaulted or became CCC rated, the structure would require a pay down of some of the higher-rated debt, shortening its life and potentially threatening the hedge fund's investment. As corporate defaults rose in the recession of 2008, this feature became increasingly problematic for many CLOs.

Overall, the CLO market existed primarily to finance corporate bank, real estate, and other select loans. If a hedge fund was not involved in these markets, this financing was of no use. Although many funds did take advantage of this market, its relatively narrow scope limited its proliferation to a fraction of the size of traditional prime brokerage or term bank hedge fund financing markets.

As it has with many other forms of commercial and consumer financing, the credit crisis has effectively eliminated hedge fund access to both CLO financing and medium-term notes. Down the road it is possible that they will reemerge but with significantly less aggressive structures.

Leverage Covenants—Hedge Fund Trip Wires

All leverage utilized by hedge funds contains contractual covenants. Covenants protect the lenders by requiring the fund to maintain certain objective levels of security-by-security margin, fund AUM, performance, leverage, and other parameters. These covenants also include, in some cases, other subjective tests that can provide the lender with an exit, even when the objective tests are met by the borrower.

Each financing facility—prime brokerage agreements, term bank facilities, repos, swaps, or other derivative instruments that contain embedded financing—tends to have a covenant package that is unique to both the facility and the bank/counterparty that arranged it. Given the wide array of financing facilities, banks, and counterparties involved in a typical leveraged hedge fund, most financing providers insist on the inclusion of a "cross default" provision. Under a cross default covenant, if there is a significant default in one financing facility, it creates a default in *all* financings that are subject to the cross default feature.

As a result, a leveraged hedge fund is only as strong as the weakest covenant in any of its financing facilities. This provides protection for the banks by bringing all creditors to the table simultaneously, but it also creates more risk for the fund by increasing the chance of it defaulting all of its debt capital at once.

Know Your ISDA

In order to maintain some level of order among the many hedge fund financing agreements, many larger, established managers have migrated toward a single set of covenants that serve as a core set of rules to be referenced by each of the fund's many financing agreements. These covenants are contained in the fund's ISDA (International Swap Dealers Association) agreements.

ISDA agreements are important for a couple of reasons. First, they serve as the industry's standard covenants for most major financing facilities, including prime brokerage and term bank facilities. Additionally, over-the-counter derivative securities (swaps, futures, options, etc.) are almost exclusively governed by ISDA agreements. These instruments now represent *trillions* of dollars of collective hedge fund exposure, forming a daisy chain of risk that runs through banks, broker-dealers, hedge funds, and other counterparties in the form of investments, hedges, and "back to back" swap agreements that are used to transfer risk from institution to institution. In short, those who have mastered the key details of their fund's ISDA language know where most of the trip wires are hidden.

The three objective covenants that are most likely to be violated in hedge fund financing agreements are (1) the margin maintenance requirements, (2) the net asset value (NAV) trigger, and (3) "key man" provisions, which govern the loss or behavior of key personnel within the fund.

Margin Maintenance

When a bank or prime broker provides a fund with leverage to purchase a security, the fund is required to maintain, on a daily basis, a certain percentage of cash collateral, or "haircut," against the position. The mechanics of this maintenance are fairly straightforward: Let's say a fund purchases a $1,000 bond with a 10% haircut. The fund is required to post $100 cash to secure the dealer's $900 of leverage which together total the $1,000 needed to purchase the bond. Now imagine that on the following day the market price of the bond drops to 95%, leaving the fund with only $50 of collateral remaining ($950 bond value minus $900 loan). In order to maintain its 10% margin requirement, the fund must post an additional $45 to raise its margin to a total of $95, or 10% of the new market price. Should the price of the bond go up, the dealer would be required to return additional cash into the hedge fund's account.

In general, haircut levels are established on both a security-by-security and protfolio basis in a fund's financing agreement. Factors that affect the levels include the risk of the particular investment, the perception of overall market risk at any given time, and competing levels set by other dealers. Mathematically, the difference between the haircut and the purchase price is equal to the amount of leverage that the bank or prime broker provides. If you need to determine the leverage multiple, you simply take the inverse of the haircut ratio (i.e., a 10% haircut equates to 10 times leverage on the underlying cash margin posting).

Before the credit crisis, minimum haircut levels range from as little as 5% or 10% to over 50%. Typical levels were 20% for unhedged long or short equity positions (five times leverage), 10% for hedged equity investments (10 times leverage), 10% for hedged convertible bonds (10 times leverage), 5% for short maturity A-rated bonds (20 times leverage), 50% for distressed or defaulted bonds (2 times leverage), and so on. By mid-2009, the amount of leverage offered through this type of bank and prime brokerage margin financing had been reduced by 50% or more for many securities.

If the fund fails to maintain this specified level of collateral for each security on a daily basis, it is in default. If, after a grace period of a few days, the fund is unable to cure the default by selling securities to raise cash or adding cash to its account, the dealer will simply start selling the fund's positions in the open market. Importantly, if these sales are not adequate to satisfy the deficit, then the dealer has a claim on all other assets of the hedge fund until the deficit is cured. This is known in the industry as "full recourse" financing.

In addition to traditional margin requirements, most financing agreements also require a fund to maintain certain parameters that effectively regulate the design of its investment portfolio. In particular, these covenants establish maximum levels of position, industry, and country concentration, as well as minimum liquidity levels for investments. For most funds, sound overall portfolio management will ensure that most of these levels are routinely met.

The NAV Trigger

Another important covenant embedded in hedge fund financing facilities is the NAV, or net asset value, trigger. This covenant creates a default and possible termination of the financing facility if the net asset value (the market value of all of a fund's investments, less the face value of the debt it owes) of the fund declines below a specified level. This covenant typically states that the financing facility will default if a fund's NAV drops by a specified percentage over a specified period of time, e.g., 10% or 15% in a month, 15% or 20% in a quarter, and 25% or 30% in a year. Surprisingly, in many covenant packages, both the inflows and outflows (redemptions) of investor capital *and* the investment performance of the fund determine the NAV. As a result, even if a fund has a six month term financing facility, all of that financing will terminate if performance declines and/or investor redemptions cause the fund's NAV to drop below these levels.

If a NAV trigger is in danger of being tripped by a redemption-driven decline in NAV, many hedge funds have a mechanism that can help. This feature is called the fund's "gate." The gate serves to limit investor withdrawals during a certain period to a percentage of fund assets; typically withdrawals are prohibited from rising above 15% or 20% in any quarter. By keeping the amount of redemptions at a level beneath the NAV trigger, the fund can prevent a bank or financing counterparty from grabbing control of its "steering wheel" and initiating a fire sale of the portfolio. (The gate feature is described in more detail in Chapter 6.)

By "putting up the gate," a fund can ensure that it doesn't trip the NAV trigger as a result of investor redemptions alone. Remember, however, that this covenant is often triggered by a reduction in NAV from either investor withdrawals *or* poor performance. Thus, if a fund loses more than 5% in a month and receives 15% redemptions (for a total monthly drop in NAV over 20%), a 15% gate may not be able prevent a default or termination event from occurring.

In general, the gate is not designed to drive the wolf from the door. It may prevent a default temporarily, but its main function is to buy the fund time. In many cases, a gate event will beget even more redemptions, increasing the probability that the NAV trigger will be tripped a quarter or two down the road.

The Key Man Provision

This covenant gives the bank or prime broker the option to terminate a financing facility if any previously designated key personnel leave or are indicted for fraud or any other crime that could have an adverse effect on the fund. As with margin requirements and the NAV trigger, if key man provisions are violated and a default is declared, the dealer has the right, after a very short cure period, to liquidate the investments of the fund.

In practice, banks are reluctant to resort to asset liquidations when a default occurs. By doing so, they risk putting themselves in the position of a distressed seller of unfamiliar assets. In such a fire sale, the prices they might fetch would likely be dramatically lower than those on the current market, which in turn could threaten the banks' own recovery levels. In spite of these risks, banks and prime brokers have exercised this right in cases of extreme stress and undoubtedly will continue to do so in the future.

The Dreaded Subjective Covenants

In addition to these objective tests of creditworthiness, banks and prime brokers sometimes include other more subjective covenants. One such test is the "adequate assurances" covenant. This provides that at any time, a dealer can call for additional collateral (cash or other assets) from a fund in order to "assure" the dealer that it is adequately protected. With covenant language this vague, almost any period of real stress could trigger a breach, causing a default and possible liquidation of collateral. Of course, the fund is welcome to argue the dealer's interpretation afterward, but it will probably do so from the bridge of a sunken ship.

Another highly subjective covenant included in some hedge fund financings is the "public source" event. This test states that if a public source—CNBC or the *Wall Street Journal*, for example— reports that the fund is in severe distress, the dealer can declare a default, seize collateral, and begin to liquidate. Importantly, under this covenant, dealers can take these steps before receiving the fund's official monthly performance report to confirm the rumored distress.

For banks and prime brokers, these more subjective covenants are highly desirable. They provide fast-track protection for their collateral by avoiding the time-consuming process of verifying the fund's actual losses and accompanying NAV decline through normal monthly fund performance reporting.

For hedge funds, on the other hand, both of these subjective covenants are highly problematic. Given that almost all involuntary auctions of hedge fund assets end badly for investors, these poorly defined, subjective tests expose a fund and its investors to a risk that is both hard to predict and difficult to control. As a result, hedge fund managers have increasingly pushed to keep these provisions out of financing agreements.

An Unwanted Trip to the Barber

Another maddening worry exists for hedge funds that are heavy users of term prime brokerage financing. In times of stress, many prime brokers have been known to unilaterally raise a fund's margin (haircut) requirements and funding costs without going through the normal multimonth "term-out" process outlined in their prime brokerage agreement. In the fall of 2008, prime brokers and banks, faced with deteriorating balance sheets, excess leverage, and a loss of traditional sources of funding, began to substantially reduce leverage allocated to hedge funds or pull the financing altogether. For the most part, this was accomplished by simply jacking up the collateral requirements for a variety of securities. Leverage for convertible securities, high-yield bonds, equities, loans, and other securities was cut across the board, in many cases by more than half. For any leverage that remained, financing rates paid by the hedge fund more than doubled, jumping from fed funds plus ~25 bps (2.25% in June 2008) to somewhere in the neighborhood of LIBOR plus 300 bps (4.50% in December 2008).

Apparently the discussions went something like this:

PRIME BROKER: "Hi. We wanted to let you know that we'll
be taking your haircuts and cost of borrowing up."

HEDGE FUND: "Really? Are you terming me out? Because I
don't think I've broken any covenants."

PRIME BROKER: "Yeah, um, like I said: we're going to be taking your haircut and costs up."

Translation: "If you don't like it, leave, and if you leave, good luck finding better terms." This left most hedge funds with three possible options: (1) accept the new terms, (2) leave for another prime broker and get stuck with similar new terms anyway, or (3) sue to enforce the contract.

However justified a lawsuit might have seemed, most funds were in no position to sue. In the midst of a violent crisis with poor returns and unstable capital, suing your prime broker in hopes of winning a judgment three years forward was like cutting your throat to stop a nose bleed. Most chose door number one, accepted the lower leverage, and moved on.

The problem, of course, was that this move forced funds to sell positions immediately to meet the tougher capital (margin) requirements—without the benefit of the contractual multimonth period over which they would normally attempt to manage such asset sales. Furthermore, this sale came at precisely the worst time, when everyone else was also being forced to sell. As Figure 2-1 shows, the actions of prime brokers in late 2008 shut down the hedge fund leverage party like parents walking into a high school beer blast.

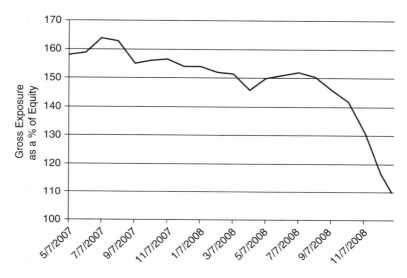

Figure 2-1 Historical leverage levels for equity long-short funds, May 2007 to January 2009
Source: Prime brokerage data

The Prime Broker Black Hole

Until recently, most hedge fund managers probably spent very little time analyzing the ramifications of a bankruptcy at their prime broker. This complacency came to an abrupt end following the fire sale of Bear Stearns and the collapse of Lehman Brothers. Lehman's fall was a particularly nasty shock. As a result of its bankruptcy filing, hedge funds, which were either financing assets at Lehman's prime broker or allowing that unit to "rehypothecate," or lend their securities to other investors, unexpectedly became general creditors in the liquidation, limiting the potential recovery of their holdings to as little as 20 cents on the dollar.

Wait a minute, you say. How do privately owned assets, which are simply being held or financed at a prime broker, suddenly get lost and viewed as collateral for creditors of the Lehman Brothers holding company? The answer lies in the unique way that Lehman structured the firm. At most prime brokers, custody of client assets and financing is typically done at a U.S.-domiciled, regulated broker-dealer. In the event of a bankruptcy, client cash, securities, and other assets remain the property of the underlying investor and are fully accessible at market value. At Lehman Brothers, however, the U.S. prime brokerage unit financed some client positions through its London-based Lehman Brothers International Europe (LBIE) unit. By establishing an offshore broker-dealer, Lehman was able to avoid certain U.S. regulations that limited leverage and security rehypothecation, thus allowing Lehman to provide more aggressive terms to its clients.

Unfortunately for these investors, this also meant that their securities, cash, and other assets were held and financed outside of Lehman's U.S.-regulated broker-dealer unit. As a result, when the company filed for bankruptcy, investors lost the normal protections associated with accounts held in a U.S.-regulated broker-dealer; they were regarded as general creditors of the parent company. The courts viewed any investor assets at the U.K. broker-dealer as general obligations of the insolvent holding company, and this meant investors had little hope of recovering their capital.

To date, a number of investors, including Ramius Capital[2] and Diamondback Capital Management,[3] among others, have warned of assets stranded at Lehman. How many of these funds fully understood the subtlety of U.S. versus international broker-dealer risk is unclear. Whatever the hedge funds might have known, "black hole" bankruptcy structures are yet another reason prime brokerage financing tends to be least secure at times when stability is most important.

Leveraging Historical Returns

In the years preceding the credit crisis, the constant flow of capital into hedge funds rose to one record high after another. As increasingly more capital chased the same pool of assets, prices rose and expected investment returns declined. This in turn created more demand for leverage as funds sought to continue to generate returns that would justify a 2% and 20% fee structure.

For many hedge funds, particularly credit-oriented or multi-strategy funds, the higher use of leverage required portfolio hedges that could keep pace with the increased risk. In addition, the hedges had to provide protection at a cost that preserved most of the returns inherent in the strategy. To pull this off, the short hedge exposure established in a particular security or derivative needed to generate substantially more profit in a down market than the asset being hedged would lose. In this way, the fund could purchase a lower dollar amount of the hedge, creating less drag on the fund's return, and still report to its investors that it was "fully hedged." Examples of this strategy include hedging senior debt of a company with subordinated debt of the same company, or hedging a highly rated basket of securities with a lower rated but very similar basket.

One of the more popular strategies that fit this description was leveraged hedge fund investments in corporate bank loans. For decades, corporate bank loans were primarily the domain of banks themselves; banks structured them, priced them, and, for the most part, held them on their books. Starting in the late 1990s, however, they became more and more an institutionally owned product, thanks to the advent of CLOs, the explosive increase of leveraged loan issuance in connection with private equity LBOs, and the hedge funds' growing appetite for bank loan exposure. Many hedge funds viewed this type of investment as inherently low risk: it was the most senior part of the capital structure, secured by the assets of the company, and had a years-long track record of very low volatility. Furthermore, there were ample opportunities to establish hedges that would meet the objectives discussed above.

With this investment thesis in mind, more than a few hedge fund managers confidently pursued strategies that targeted purchasing noninvestment grade (typically single B rated) senior secured bank loans, financed with roughly 60% to 80% leverage and 20% to 40% equity capital. The hedge of choice for many managers was subordinated high-yield debt, typically in the form of individual bonds or a broad index hedge, against the portfolio. Because high yield had historically declined by three to five times as much as bank debt in times of stress, a hedge fund could hedge any potential decline in the bank loan market with a hedge equal to only 20% to 33% of a loan portfolio's dollar amount. Assuming this performance held in future market downturns, a fund could claim to be fully hedged while paying out only a fraction of its return in hedging costs. Very clever, if it worked.

Unfortunately for these strategists, it didn't work particularly well. When the first wave of the credit tsunami hit in the summer of 2007, loan prices started to tank; soon they were trading lower than they had in 20 years. Making matters worse, the assumptions that many hedge funds had made about the relative underperformance of

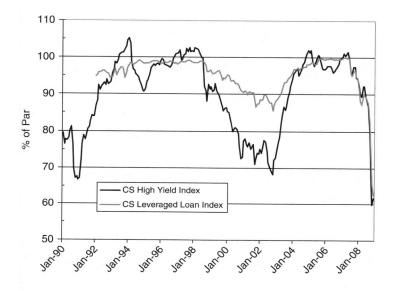

Figure 2-2 Credit Suisse High Yield Index vs. Credit Suisse Leveraged Loan Index, 1990 to 2008
Source: Bloomberg

high yield in downturns proved to be flawed. In fact, high yield was declining in lockstep with bank debt, which meant that most hedge funds were significantly under hedged on a highly leveraged investment (see Figure 2-2).

In letters to their investors, many shocked hedge fund managers characterized the price moves as "unprecedented." Even Standard & Poor's seemed to agree; in January 2008, it described the decline in the loan market as a "six standard deviation move."

Statistically speaking, a six standard deviation event has roughly a one-in-a-billion chance of occurring—about as likely, in other words, as your being subject to an alien abduction before you finish this chapter. However fuzzy the analysts' math was, the decline had happened against expectations, and it exposed a flaw common to hedge funds: the tendency to overutilize leverage and minimize the consequences of underperforming, critical, "historically correlated" hedges.

The recent collapse of Sowood Capital Management and the Bear Stearns hedge funds are both case studies in this regard. They are also particularly good examples of the perils associated with financing longer-duration, less-liquid assets with short-term, covenant-heavy debt.

The Collapse of Sowood Capital Management

Sowood Capital Management was founded in 2004 by Jeff Larson, a former senior portfolio manager at Harvard Management, the investment arm that oversees Harvard University's endowment. During his nearly 13 years at Harvard, he successfully managed approximately $3 billion of capital spread across portfolios filled with international equities, commodities, and other investments. By all accounts, Larson built a stellar track record at the endowment, consistently outperforming most major investment benchmarks. His pay at Harvard, which reportedly totaled as much as $17 million a year,[4] seemed to confirm his status as an investment superstar.

When Larson left the endowment to start Sowood, the university committed $500 million to the new fund. This investment, coupled with his reputation as a major talent in the asset management business, made Sowood a relatively easy sell to new investors. Over its first three years, the fund's performance was attractive, consistently generating net annual returns of around 10%. This performance, coupled with the gleam provided by Harvard's imprimatur, attracted a steady stream of capital; by 2007, Sowood had $3 billion in AUM.[5]

A multi-strategy fund, Sowood engaged in a variety of investment strategies including relative value credit, equity investments, convertible arbitrage, risk arbitrage, commodity trading, and others. Like similarly structured funds of the time, Sowood used large chunks of borrowed money to amplify the returns of many of these strategies.

The relative value credit strategy was an area that involved particularly high levels of leverage. It was in this portfolio that Sowood implemented its strategy of buying senior secured corporate bank loans and hedging itself with a combination of subordinated high-yield debt (most likely via bonds and credit default swaps) and equity put options.[6] Sowood reportedly leveraged these positions by as much as six times the firm's capital.[7]

This investment expressed a view that Sowood shared with many other funds at the time. When the credit bubble was at its apex in early 2007, many believed the market was due for a correction and that the safest haven for investments would be senior bank debt secured by the assets of the underlying company. They also believed that riskier, subordinated high-yield debt was due for a fall and expected it to mirror its performance in previous downturns (see Figure 2-2). Perhaps most important, this strategy satisfied a hedge fund's desire to generate the consistent low-volatility returns prized by investors while maintaining a hedged portfolio.

For this, senior secured bank loans provided the perfect vehicle: they paid consistent interest each month, usually 2% to 3% over LIBOR (many of the loans were issued to support leveraged buyouts by private equity sponsors and tended to be noninvestment grade, single B rated loans), and they had a history of price stability. As highlighted in Figure 2-2, for more than 15 years the CS Leveraged Loan Index rarely traded below 90% of par. Furthermore, because the loans were both senior and secured by the assets of the issuer, recovery was expected to be substantial even if a company filed for bankruptcy.

If that wasn't a sufficiently attractive package, by now banks and other leverage providers were high on the low-volatility Kool-Aid as well. They were willing to provide hedge funds with extraordinary levels of leverage for bank loans—even more than Sowood was already utilizing—probably maxing out at somewhere in the vicinity of 12 to 15 times, depending on the type of loans held.

Consider the hypothetical economics of six times leverage that Sowood probably modeled: Invest $167 of firm capital. Borrow $833 from a bank and purchase a bank loan with a face value of $1,000 (equal to six times the equity invested). Assume the bank loan pays LIBOR plus 2.5%, and the financing carries a cost of LIBOR plus 0.5%. A simple income calculation (assuming the market price of the loan is stable) shows that Sowood would theoretically make 2% (LIBOR + 2.5% minus LIBOR + 0.5%) on the borrowed $833, or $16.66. Add to that another $13.03 on the $167 of invested capital (2.5% plus the going LIBOR rate at the time of 5.3%), and Sowood could make a gross return of $29.69, or 17.8% on its $167 of invested capital. After deducting the fund's 2% and 20% fee structure but before incorporating the cost of hedges, it could report a 12.6% net return to its investors. Very welcome news, indeed.

With the cost of its hedges, this return would have been lower, but not significantly so. In determining the size and composition of its hedges, Sowood probably looked at some of the same data included in Figure 2-2 and concluded what many others had: in down markets, high yield will always significantly underperform bank debt. In each of the last two recession years — 1991 and 2002 — high-yield debt experienced declines of 20% to 30% versus declines of 5% to 10% or less in the bank debt market. Using these broad numbers as a guide, Sowood probably established a hedge consisting of both high-yield credit default swaps and equity put options that was short roughly $0.20 for every dollar of long exposure to bank loans. If bank loans, high yield, and equity each performed as they had in previous downturns, Sowood would be more than adequately hedged.

Going back to the earlier example, if Sowood used $200 of high-yield credit default swaps and equity put options to hedge each $1,000 investment in bank loans, it would have added about $6 of hedging costs, reducing the gross return of the investment from $29.69 to $23.69. Even with this cost, the investment would still have produced a net return of approximately 10% for each $167 of equity invested, easily maintaining the historical net returns of the fund.

It's doubtful that all these rosy calculations have kept you from guessing how the movie ended. In June 2007, the price of bank loans began to slip, which caused Sowood's investments to drop a reported 5%. Despite this setback, the fund was still up for the year. Not only did Larson stick with the strategy, he apparently invested over $5 million more of his own money in the fund and directed his portfolio managers effectively to double down. Leverage was jacked up to as much as 12 times the firm's capital.[8]

The price of bank debt continued its decline in July, dropping nearly 5%. The rub for Sowood was that the price of subordinated debt did not follow history's lead; instead of plummeting, it declined by an amount approximately equal to bank debt. Equities were up midway through the month. If Sowood's high-yield and equity put hedges covered only 20% of the loan portfolio, then, given their performance, at least 80% of the portfolio was unhedged.

If these assumptions are correct, the math is easy to calculate, and painful. On a $1,000 loan, they lost 5%, or $50. After the $10 of gains from their hedge (5% decline on a $200 short position), they lost $40. On any low leverage or unlevered portfolio, this loss would have been manageable. But with more than 10 times leverage, their capital loss on the bank loan investments would have theoretically been more than 40%.

Fortunately for Sowood, their equity investors were locked up until the end of 2008; whatever panic they might have been feeling, they were trapped. But it was a different story with Sowood's banks, prime brokers, and other lenders. As the value of the fund's investments dropped, the bank's daily margin requirements, discussed earlier in this chapter, would have necessitated that Sowood post more collateral. To do this, they needed to either sell assets or raise new cash.

Unfortunately, given the heavy use of leverage by other bank loan investors, they were not the only ones looking to sell. As a result, liquidity in the loan market was becoming increasingly scarce. To make matters worse, Sowood's other investments were bound to experience a decline in both price and liquidity as soon as word of its troubles was out. With all these factors working against it, the fund would have been hard-pressed to raise needed cash through asset sales in the brief time available.

With the banks' patience probably running thin, Larson turned to Harvard for an additional equity investment or a line of credit. The university denied both requests.[9] By the end of July, the fund was down by more than 40%. Given the magnitude of this loss, there is a good chance that the fund was in violation of its NAV bank covenant. Facing a possible ultimatum from its banks, with no access to new equity capital and an increasingly illiquid loan market, Sowood apparently had two unpalatable choices: seek a fire sale bid for the assets or let the banks seize the portfolio and sell it themselves.

Given those circumstances, Larson probably reasoned that leaving the responsibility for selling securities to a less sophisticated staff at a bank—which would be unfamiliar with the fund's investments—was the greater evil. Instead, he sold off the majority of Sowood's portfolio to Citadel Investment Group, a Chicago-based hedge fund run by Ken Griffin. Although the terms of that sale were not disclosed, it is known that Sowood reported losses of 53% and 57% for its two funds during the month of July and over 50% for both for the year (bear in mind that these figures include the sale of the portfolio to Citadel).

In a letter to investors, Jeffrey Larson outlined the situation and Sowood's decision to close.

July 30, 2007

To Our Investors in Sowood Alpha Fund LP and Sowood Alpha Fund Ltd.:

Sale of Assets

Today we made the painful and difficult decision to sell substantially all the funds' portfolio to Citadel Investment Group. We took this step to protect your investment.

Our actions over the weekend followed severe declines in the value of our credit positions and non-performance of offsetting hedges. Given what we were facing and our uncertain ability to meet margin calls, we sought other buyers for some or all of the positions. Citadel offered the only immediate and comprehensive solution. The transaction enabled us to avoid anticipated forced sales at extreme prices that would have been made in order to satisfy obligations under our counterparty agreements.

Performance Update

After the transaction with Citadel, the Net Asset Value (NAV) of Sowood Alpha Fund Ltd. and Sowood Alpha Fund LP will have declined approximately 57% and 53% month to date respectively, and approximately 56% and 51% calendar year to date respectively. As a result, our NAV as of July 30 is approximately $1.5 billion.

The letter went on to describe the rationale for Sowood's decision to sell to Citadel: sharply lower prices, margin calls from financing counterparties, and limited market liquidity for the assets they held.

During the month of June, our portfolio experienced losses mostly as a result of sharply wider corporate credit spreads unaccompanied by any concomitant move in equities and exacerbated by a marked decline in liquidity. This occurred over a broad range of credit related instruments. In the first two weeks of July, spreads continued to widen, and we experienced a loss similar to June. The weakness in corporate credit—particularly focused on loans and loan credit default swaps—accelerated sharply during the week of July 23. Until the end of last week these developments, while reducing the value of our portfolio, were manageable. Our counterparties had not severely marked down the value of the collateral that the funds had posted nor changed our margin terms, and immediate liquidity needs could be met.

However, towards the end of last week, given the extreme market volatility, our counterparties began to severely mark down the value of the collateral that had been posted by the funds. In addition, liquidity became extremely limited for the credit portion of our portfolio making it difficult to exit positions. We, therefore, reached the conclusion over the weekend that, in the interest of preserving our investors' capital, the appropriate course of action was to sell the funds' portfolio. We believe that the arrangement with Citadel provided our best option under the circumstances, since we were unable to find other sources of liquidity.

Larsen ended the letter with something highly uncharacteristic in an industry accustomed to years of uninterrupted success: an apology.

We are very sorry this has happened. We have always attempted to do the very best for our investors. A loss of this magnitude in such a short period is as devastating to us as it is to you. We are committed to acting in the best interests of the funds' investors and to keeping investors informed of decisions made in furtherance of this objective.

We sincerely appreciate your patience and understanding during this challenging period.

Sincerely,

Jeff Larson

Given the circumstances, the sale to Citadel, as painful as it was for investors, was probably the best decision Larson could have made. The CS Leveraged Loan Index continued to slide, finally bottoming out in December 2008, at a price approximately 35% lower than it was at the time of Larson's decision to sell. Had he somehow managed to hold on until then, the outcome might have been substantially worse.

In hindsight, Sowood had all of the elements required for a catastrophic blowup: high leverage, illiquid investments, and hedges that not only *assumed* a predetermined correlation with the investment but in fact *required* that correlation in order to survive. Sowood, of course, was not the only fund ensnared in this trap. If there is a twist to Sowood's story, it's probably not that disaster struck, but that it struck one of the most talented and experienced managers in the business.

Leverage Strikes Again: The Bear Stearns Hedge Fund Debacle

Excessive leverage struck again in 2007, when, in the span of just a few weeks, two hedge funds managed by Bear Stearns collapsed, resulting in a complete loss for all investors in the funds. Remarkably, the two funds in question, the Bear Stearns High-Grade Structured Credit Strategies Master Fund (the High-Grade Fund) and the High-Grade Structured Credit Strategies Enhanced Leverage Master Fund (the Enhanced Fund) were designed to provide conservative "money market"–like returns and specifically avoided trying to hit "home runs."

Ralph Cioffi was the founder and senior portfolio manager of both the High-Grade and Enhanced Funds. A 1978 graduate of

Vermont's Saint Michael's College, Cioffi joined Bear Stearns in 1985 as a bond salesman and quickly rose through the ranks to become head of fixed income sales by 1989.[10] As the market for collateralized debt obligations (CDOs), asset-backed securities, and other structured products grew, Cioffi increasingly steered Bear into the sales, trading, and origination of these instruments. In 2003, he reportedly considered leaving Bear Stearns to start his own CDO-focused hedge fund.

Rather than let him go, Bear's senior management kept him in the fold by allowing him to launch his fund out of the firm's asset management division. In the fall of that year, he unveiled the High-Grade Fund.[11] While marketing his creation, Cioffi described the investment strategy as targeted toward low-risk, high-grade debt securities, primarily AAA- and AA-rated tranches of CDOs.[12] A CDO is a security, much like the CLOs discussed earlier in this chapter, whose payment of interest and principal is backed by a pool of other debt instruments, typically mortgages or other corporate debt securities. In the case of the High-Grade Fund, Cioffi focused on investments in CDOs that were backed primarily by subprime (lower credit quality) residential mortgages.

These CDOs represented a complex daisy chain of risk that usually began with securities called residential mortgaged-backed securities (RMBS). To create an RMBS, an asset manager (typically not an end investor like Bear Stearns) would purchase a large pool of subprime residential mortgages. Against that pool of mortgages, the manager would issue a number of tranches of new debt. The highest tranche of the "stack" was the most secure because it was the last tranche to lose interest payments or principal if the underlying homeowners defaulted on their mortgages.

These securities were typically rated AAA by the rating agencies; in other words, the agencies considered them to be about as safe as the U.S. government or GE. As a result, the AAA slice paid the lowest return of all of the tranches. From there, as the risk assumed by the investors increased, the ratings assigned to each successively riskier tranche declined (AA, A, and BBB, etc.), and the returns paid to investors stepped up accordingly. The equity tranche, at the bottom of the stack, usually accounted for roughly 5% or less of the RMBS capital; since it was the first to lose interest and principal if the underlying mortgages defaulted, it was therefore the riskiest of all tranches sold.

Incredibly, when all of this structuring magic was complete, approximately 90% of these RMBS tranches typically received an investment-grade rating, even though subprime mortgages are themselves not considered investment-grade securities.

The RMBS was just one step in the process. In order to create more diversification among the underlying mortgages, an investment bank would seek to create a new pool with different debt tranches from hundreds of RMBS deals. With this second pool of securities they would create a new subprime CDO, which functioned just like the RMBS structure except that the underlying collateral was the debt of RMBS deals, not direct subprime residential mortgages. The CDO then issued more AAA, AA, and BBB tranches of new debt collateralized by the pool of RMBS debt.

Once again, the rating agencies looked at all of this slicing, dicing, packaging, and repackaging and were pleased with what they saw. The agencies' models concluded that with the increased diversification that accompanied the pooling of many different RMBS deals, the majority of the debt issued by the CDO (and backed by RMBS tranches) could be given the seal of quasi-U.S. government quality: AAA and AA ratings. And, remarkably, over 90% of all tranches typically received an investment-grade rating.

Cioffi wasn't apparently concerned by all this structuring alchemy; by all accounts, he was a true believer. As head of fixed income at Bear, he directed the sales and trading efforts of the firm toward these securities, with great success. When he left the sales and trading world in 2003 to start the fund, it was only natural that he would invest the majority of his new capital in CDOs and other structured securities. His specific area of focus was the "safe" AAA- and AA-rated subprime residential mortgage CDO tranches.

For the first several years, the flagship High-Grade Fund did very well. It recorded 40 straight months of positive returns[13] and amassed over $1.5 billion in AUM. In order to generate its targeted double-digit returns, the fund levered itself aggressively, reportedly borrowing as much as 10 times the amount of its equity capital through repo agreements and other short-term borrowings. The rationale for this level of leverage was most likely a function of economic necessity: In order to generate a net return of 12% after 2% management and 20% performance fees on an asset that pays just 1.0% to 1.5% over LIBOR, you need a lot of leverage. For most of 2006, LIBOR was roughly 5.5%. Assuming a yield on the fund's CDO tranche investments of around LIBOR plus 1.25%, the fund could make roughly 6.75% without any leverage. Unfortunately, after fees, this produced a paltry net annual return to investors of just 3.8%.

And so back we go to the leverage buffet. Through its repo agreements, the fund probably borrowed at a cost of roughly

5.25% in 2006. Like Sowood, if the fund leveraged its CDO debt investments 10 to 1, for every $1,000 loan, it would need to invest $100 of its investor capital and then borrow the remaining $900. The fund would make 1.5% (6.75% of income minus the 5.25% financing cost) on the $900, or $13.50. Add to that another 6.75% or $6.75 on the $100 of invested capital and Cioffi's team would make a gross return of $20.25, or 20.25%, on its $100 of invested capital. Take away the 2% management fee and 20% incentive fee that the fund charged and voila: the fund could report a 14.6% net return to its investors—assuming, of course, that no hedges were utilized in the portfolio to protect against declines in the subprime market.

However, like Sowood, Cioffi did utilize hedges. The High-Grade Fund reportedly utilized both customized and ABX index hedges,[14] which were designed to synthetically replicate the performance of different tranches of mortgage-backed securities, from AAA to BBB. Like the credit default contracts that Sowood likely used, the ABX is structured as a swap, so it required no financing. Cioffi most likely utilized the ABX BBB tranches as the fund's primary hedge, which would have cost the fund approximately 1.75% for each dollar of short exposure. Going back to the previous example, if the fund hedged using $200 (or 20% of its long investment) of short BBB exposure, the gross return would have been reduced by $3.50 (1.75% of $200) to 16.75% before fees, which equates to just under a 12% net return (after fees) to investors—more or less the target of the fund.

The theory behind this hedge, in many ways, paralleled the Sowood strategy. Cioffi and his risk team probably wagered that if AAA and AA tranches of subprime CDO paper declined, then the

BBB tranches would decline by multiples of the higher-rated tranches. Once again, this would have been a cheap way to "hedge" the portfolio if you assumed that both the longs and the shorts behaved as the risk management models dictated they would. Unfortunately for Cioffi and his team, betting the survival of the fund on a hedge that, in order to be effective, required a specific, predetermined correlation with the fund's long investments, was a high-stakes bet. And, like Sowood, they lost.

In mid-2006, the assets of the High-Grade Fund peaked at just over $1.5 billion. Around this time, Cioffi opened a new entity, the Enhanced Fund,[15] which would seek to generate enhanced returns through—believe it or not—even more leverage, eventually reaching the ludicrous heights of 17 *times* the capital of the fund (long investments divided by investor capital).[16]

Quite a hard sell, one would think. To assuage investor concerns about the fund's extraordinary use of leverage, the Enhanced Fund restricted its investments to largely higher-quality AAA-rated securities. Hard as it may be to believe, in hindsight, the fund succeeded in raising more than $600 million of capital, although some of it was reportedly cannibalized from the High-Grade Fund.

Unfortunately for Bear, the warm glow of this promising launch would fade in a matter of months. From August 2006 until January 2007, the fund reported positive monthly returns, despite a weakening market for mortgage-related investments. By the end of February, though, a new reality was settling in. The High-Grade Fund reported a gain of approximately 1%, but the Enhanced Fund reported a decline of 0.8% for the month, the first loss ever reported by either of Cioffi's funds.[17]

Despite the relatively modest size of this dip, the prospects for the fund were becoming increasingly grim. In the mortgage market, housing prices were declining, default rates were climbing, and a wave of rate resets on adjustable-rate mortgages (ARMs) was threatening to dramatically accelerate default levels. After a decade of excess in the housing market, the problem would grow to epic proportions: the total value of subprime mortgages outstanding had ballooned to $1.3 trillion, up from just $35 billion in 1994. The median down payment for first-time home buyers had slipped to just 2%, with 43% of those buyers making no down payment whatsoever. And subprime ARMs—which allowed homeowners to pay an initial teaser rate of below 3% for a year or two before stepping up to 6% to 8%+ thereafter—were starting to go bad in a big way, with default levels up nearly 100% versus 2005.

In the Enhanced Fund, the math underlying the February performance numbers was troubling. The market value of subprime CDO investments in the Enhanced Fund had declined by14.4%, an alarming monthly number for securities that retained their AAA ratings. This disastrous loss was covered by the fund's hedges (short the ABX subprime index and other derivative hedges), which produced a lifesaving gain of roughly 13.6%.

The High-Grade Fund, with its lower leverage, saw its long CDO assets marked down by 4.4%, but it had managed to report a profitable month because its ABX hedges produced a profit of roughly 5.3%.[18]

In March and April, the pressure on subprime CDO investments continued. With the value of these assets plummeting, the Enhanced Fund's fate rested in the continued performance of the fund's ABX hedges. From a risk management perspective, the steep decline in AAA-rated CDO assets had already put the fund in a bad scenario that its risk models would have deemed highly unlikely. Now, mired in this improbable position, the fund's risk models assumed that its hedges would continue to behave rationally and in keeping with historical averages. Given the amount of leverage the fund was carrying, these risk management assumptions left little room for error; the fund needed the hedges to maintain their precise historical correlation at *precisely* the moment in time when stress levels in the market were most severe.

Unfortunately for Cioffi, all these assumptions proved to be very flawed indeed. In April, the performance of the fund's hedges began to decouple from the performance of the long CDO investments, squeezing the fund from both sides. The fund's CDO bonds were falling in value, and its ABX hedges were no longer performing as expected. Now the fund was in an even more unenviable position: long, highly leveraged, and ineffectively hedged. When the dust had settled, the official April performance for the Enhanced Fund was set at −18.97%, a number which would have incited near panic among the fund's already nervous investors and lenders.

On June 14, the fund's creditors convened at Bear's offices for an update. They were told that the two funds were facing a total of more than $200 million in margin calls.[19] With market liquidity for subprime CDO debt limited, the banks soon gauged the depth of the trouble. In order to be repaid, their CDO collateral and the collateral of nearly a dozen other lenders would have to be sold very quickly. Effectively, they were all facing the prospect of pushing a large volume of asset sales through a very small hole. As the meeting ended, it was clear that there were only two real alternatives: Bear Stearns needed to put up additional capital to rescue the funds, or the banks would seize the assets that served as collateral for their loans and begin selling it in the market.

The following week, Cioffi came back with a proposal: Bear would step up with as much as $2 billion of new capital for the funds if the banks would accept a 12-month moratorium on margin calls. For most of the banks, this was a nonstarter; considering the volatility and uncertainty surrounding these securities, 12 months was a lifetime. Some threw up their hands at this point. Merrill Lynch and J.P. Morgan each seized the fund's CDO investments and began the process of auctioning the assets in the market.[20]

When the bids came in from the Merrill auction, they were significantly lower than many expected and lower than Merrill was willing to accept. Chaos ensued. Several other banks started seeking bids in the marketplace while others went back to Bear to negotiate private deals. Given the leverage the funds were utilizing, a decline of 10% or more would wipe out their investors. With limited market liquidity and an ad hoc liquidation of fund assets under way, that threshold was easily breached; both funds collapsed, rendering limited partner (LP) investments effectively worthless.

In the weeks that followed, investors received a letter that attempted to explain what had happened.

Dear Client of Bear, Stearns & Co. Inc.

Let me take this opportunity to provide you with an update on the High-Grade Structured Credit Strategies and High-Grade Structured Credit Strategies Enhanced Leverage Funds . . .

As you know, in early June, the Funds were faced with investor redemption requests and margin calls that they were unable to meet. The Funds sold assets in an attempt to raise liquidity, but were unable to generate sufficient cash to meet the outstanding margin obligations. As a result, counterparties moved to seize collateral or otherwise terminate financing arrangements they had with the Funds. During June, the Funds experienced significant declines in the value of their assets resulting in losses of net asset value. The Funds' performance, in part, reflects the unprecedented declines in the valuations of a number of highly rated (AAA and AA) securities.

Fund managers and account executives have been informing the Funds' investors of the significant deterioration in performance for May and June. The preliminary estimates show that there is effectively no value left for the investors in the Enhanced Leverage Fund and very little value left for the investors in the High-Grade Fund as of June 30, 2007.

Having gotten this extraordinarily bad news out of the way, the letter closed with a shameless appeal for more business:

Throughout this time, we have appreciated the support of our loyal client base and we will continue to provide you with the high quality products and services you have come to expect from Bear Stearns . . .

Ultimately, the story behind the fall of Sowood and Bear, notwithstanding all the complex instruments and strategies, is relatively simple. They used excessive leverage to magnify small, apparently stable returns, and they utilized a historically correlated index as a hedge. In times of stress, if the performance of the hedge relative to its historical correlation data is perfect, the fund can carry on indefinitely in its game of "picking up nickels in front of an oncoming bulldozer." But if its hedge performance fails, investors will be flattened by the bulldozer.

For years prior to the collapse of the Bear funds, there was sustained debate over which hedge funds were consistently creating real alpha through the arbitrage of fundamental value discrepancies and which funds were merely producing returns through the excessive leveraging of small, seemingly stable income streams. At least for now, Bear's fund managers have been enshrined in a hall of infamy created for practitioners of the latter method.

In 2008, Ralph Cioffi and Matthew Tannin were indicted on charges of securities fraud for providing investors with allegedly inaccurate and misleading information just prior to the collapse of the funds in July 2007. It appears, however, that there was no direct causality between the Bear fund's collapse and the fraud allegations. In other words, the alleged fraud did not impact the core investment performance of the fund or contribute to its failure but was instead confined to the way in which the managers communicated the challenges they were facing. This element of the Bear Stearns story is detailed in Chapter 7.

The Fate of Hedge Fund Leverage

In the long run, as banks and prime brokers return to more stable positions, hedge fund leverage will make its inevitable comeback, but at significantly more modest levels. Arguably, this will be a net positive for the industry, since for many strategies, modest use of leverage is an advisable and prudent way to enhance certain investment opportunities. The challenge for investors, of course, will be to determine which funds can avoid the mistakes of the past and which are doomed to repeat them. To aid in that challenge, here is a list of warning signals:

- Leverage levels, even for "stable assets," exceeding three to four times investor capital
- Leverage strategies that rely heavily on "correlated hedges"
- Financing long duration assets with short-term debt
- Leveraging illiquid assets or those that have historically become illiquid in times of stress
- Subjective or unfavorable covenants
- Little or no unencumbered cash to satisfy unexpected margin calls

three

NARCISSISTIC RISK MANAGEMENT

A mid the rubble of Sowood, Bear Stearns, and the litany of other hedge fund train wrecks of 2008, many investors, with no small justification, were left wondering, "Where in god's name was the risk management process while all this was going on?" And who could blame them? Pensions, endowments, funds of funds, and individuals had poured nearly $3 trillion into hedge fund investments on the fundamental assumption that sound risk management systems were safeguarding their capital. And yet, looking back on 2008, it is painfully clear that the risk processes of many hedge funds were woefully inadequate for the world they faced. The performance sensitivity metrics and scenario analysis produced by many risk models grossly underestimated the actual risk the funds encountered; hedges that risk managers blithely assumed would work, didn't. Perhaps most frustrating, many risk processes did not even consider the most virulent threats of all: loss of financing, illiquidity, and hedge fund correlation (a phenomenon discussed in Chapter 4 that stems from overcrowded investments).

At most hedge funds, the risk management process is a collaborative effort between a risk manager and the risk committee or senior management of the fund. The risk manager typically utilizes a commercially developed risk system to produce a variety of analytics that the two groups jointly use for risk assessment, control, and predictive scenario analysis.

In most cases, risk systems produce two main pieces of information: (1) exposure analysis, which provides a snapshot of a fund's current long and short exposures, and (2) scenario analysis, a kind of "what if" testing that helps to provide a better understanding of the fund's hypothetical performance in a variety of challenging market environments.

Contrary to popular belief, these systems are not stand-alone predictive risk sages, automatically stressing each investment exposure to reveal a complete and accurate picture of the portfolio's true flaws. Instead, they are surprisingly rudimentary devices that do a good job of aggregating and monitoring basic exposures (effectively telling a fund what it owns today), but often fall well short when attempting to predict how the portfolio will perform tomorrow (i.e., scenario analysis).

This weakness is particularly pronounced in multi-strategy, credit-focused funds and other more complex portfolios. In these situations, accurate scenario analysis is possible only with meaningful modifications to the model and painstaking analytical iterations by a highly experienced risk management team. Without a world-class risk team tailoring the model to capture the real-world risks, these systems tend to revert to simplistic baseline analytics and are far more likely to underrepresent the danger inherent to the portfolio. As a result, they have a tendency to reinforce the natural expectation of any self-confident manager: "This portfolio is brilliantly designed and well positioned for good markets and bad!" The false sense of confidence created by this sort of narcissism probably contributed, at least in part, to dangerously higher tolerances for risk in the boom years of the industry.

Risk Systems 101

In its most basic form, the risk management system is a database for all of a fund's investment positions and hedges—equities, high-yield bonds, bank loans, swaps, options, futures, structured credit instruments, etc.—including a description of the key features of each: strategy designation, coupon, dividend, duration, industry, country code, and so on. When this data is linked to current market pricing, the system produces several key pieces of information:

1. Exposure data, which is a snapshot of the fund's overall long and short exposure (and leverage) broken down by strategy, industry group, security type, rating, etc.

2. Sensitivity analysis, which attempts to estimate how the fund will perform given a specified future movement in key market metrics such as credit spreads, equity prices, interest rates, levels of volatility, and so on. Most systems also attempt to simulate past periods of market turmoil—the 1987 crash, the Russian debt crisis, the tech bubble, etc.

3. Many systems also provide performance attribution by strategy, investment, or instrument. This data enables a fund to compare the performance of certain strategies or trades against the portfolio manager's original expectation for the investment.

Many funds go on to further customize these systems, adding additional metrics for enhanced analysis of a particular group of assets or perceived risks.

Arguably the most useful and probably least dangerous data these systems produce is the exposure data. This information provides both the manager and investors with a wealth of useful information: investment concentration within a certain strategy, industry, geography, security or asset type, etc.; migration of exposures over time; long and short biases; derivative exposures; a history of leverage utilization; and, through the attribution data, a road map of how the fund reacts to and manages both winning and losing positions or strategies.

For the management of a fund, this data is critical to handling the fund's overall exposures, monitoring leverage, controlling individual portfolio managers, and avoiding overlapping or conflicting positions between portfolios. For investors, this data, typically provided in aggregated form, also provides important insight into current investment strategies and the evolution of the portfolio over time.

The performance sensitivity data and scenario analysis produced by many risk models, on the other hand, can be insidiously subjective. These are generated through the use of a wide array of assumptions about the performance of the portfolio and its hedges, as well as expectations for each of the market inputs. For long-short or other portfolios focused on one or two asset classes, this type of scenario analysis is usually straightforward to produce and generally reliable. Inside multi-strategy and other multidimensional portfolios, however, the sheer number of variables and assumptions required to produce scenario analysis makes it much more art than science.

To illustrate this point, let's look at a typical, baseline sensitivity analysis. For multi-strategy and other multidimensional funds, the most commonly used benchmark sensitivity metrics include equity market sensitivity (Beta); credit and interest rate sensitivities (DV01s); Vega, a measure of sensitivity to volatility; and VaR, a measure of the total risk within a fund, to name a few.

Without modification by the risk manager, the baseline method of crunching these metrics is to vary the level of each individual market input while holding all others constant. For example, credit DV01s are typically calculated by varying the level of credit spreads in the fund's fixed income portfolio by either one basis point (1/100 of a percent) or 1% of current market spreads while holding equity prices, interest rates, volatility, exchange rates, and all other metrics constant. The total gain or loss produced by these minor variations is referred to as the fund's credit DV01. The fund's sensitivity to changes in equity is calculated in the same manner: vary the price of all equity instruments in the portfolio by 1% while holding all other market inputs constant. Additional scenarios are also run for larger percentage moves in each market.

The flaw in this type of analysis is not hard to spot. If the S&P 500 declines several percentage points, is it likely that the corresponding credit spreads and volatility of those companies will remain unchanged? If credit spreads widen dramatically, making corporate capital raising substantially more expensive and difficult, will the stock price of those companies stand still? Probably not. Without an understanding of the composition of a portfolio, it is hard to tell if these simplifying assumptions overstate or understate the risk. Either way, they limit the value of the analysis produced.

A more dangerous assumption embedded in most models involves the portfolio hedges. In the baseline analysis, most systems automatically assume that the hedges provide a "perfect" hedge to the long positions in the portfolio. Why? Because when the system calculates the impact of changes in credit spreads or equity prices to the portfolio, it applies a constant percentage change to all credit spreads and equity prices: cash long positions, short hedges, derivative contracts, etc. This means that when the prices of long positions in bonds, loans, or equities decline by 3% in the portfolio, they decline by the same amount on the short hedges and create offsetting gains. This ensures that even the most violent right and left tail events produce pain free, soft landings in a baseline performance sensitivity analysis.

For multi-strategy and other credit-focused hedge funds, this uniform approach to changes in credit spreads within the portfolio is even more problematic. These funds frequently hold large, diversified credit portfolios at every level of the corporate capital structure: senior-secured bank loans, investment-grade debt, high-yield bonds, distress debt, convertibles, CDS contracts, credit default indexes, swaps, etc. When a model produces a credit DV01, it typically changes the credit spreads of all credit instruments in the portfolio by one basis point and then calculates the impact of this change on the value of the entire portfolio. The result is usually expressed in dollars. For example, if a one basis point decrease or increase in credit spreads generates a gain or loss in the portfolio of $100,000, the manager would say that his portfolio has a DV01 of $100,000.

The problem with this standard DV01 calculation is that it tends to significantly underestimate the impact of spread changes on lower-rated securities. In calculating the DV01, the model will increase the credit spread in a high-grade bond from 100 basis points, for example, to 101 basis points, a 1% change. However, the high-yield bond spread would start from a much higher level, probably somewhere around 400 basis points, and then increase one additional basis point to 401, only a 0.25% change—a clear flaw.

Most risk managers try to solve this problem in DV01 by applying a 1% change in spreads across all instruments. For small movements in credit spreads, this certainly helps. Either way, many investors look at a credit DV01 and implicitly assume that the model's output is multiplicative. In other words, if a fund's DV01 predicts it will gain or lose $100,000 for a one basis point or 1% decline or rise in spreads, then it is assumed that the fund will gain or lose $10,000,000 for a 100 basis point move in spreads.

The relationship may in fact be linear for changes within a certain range, but when the market is stressed, the relationship between credit instruments of varying subordination tends to diverge significantly. As discussed in Chapter 2, when credit spreads widen, lower-quality spreads historically experience a telescoping effect. Spreads in the single B bank loan market will generally widen by more than those in the high-grade market, and subordinated high-yield bonds will typically widen by more than single B senior bank loans. Furthermore, for managers with distressed assets, it is very unlikely that the credit of a company in or near bankruptcy will behave like any other credit instrument.

Many managers recognize the weakness in the baseline approach and try to adjust their models to approximate their own expectations of how each different category of credit will respond to changes in a "baseline" credit spread. Some managers will hard wire their models so that a given percent change in bank loan credit spreads will impact high-yield credit spreads by two to three times as much. Some use different ratios; others don't adjust at all.

As a result, DV01s are produced and consumed in several flavors. "DV one basis point" is reasonably predictive for managers with only one type of credit instrument and mostly inaccurate for mixed credit portfolios. "DV 1%" is useful for small movements in mixed portfolios but questionable for predicting performance in periods of stress. Furthermore, whatever credit DV01 estimate is produced, it almost always assumes that every other metric, variable, and market input is held completely constant. So even while simply calculating a realistic credit DV01, a risk manager will be forced to make numerous ad hoc adjustments to account for expected changes in the equity and rate markets, volatility, variations for different levels of subordination, and other metrics. Numerous scenarios must then be run to account for the potential variation, or "basis risk," between the performance of long positions and hedges. Make all of these adjustments for each of the other sensitivity metrics and what you get, invariably, is a mountain of ambiguity.

For hedge fund managers, perhaps the most painful lesson of 2008 was that the real world, when stressed, works nothing like the theoretical framework embedded in these risk models. Hedges diverged significantly from their expected performance, bond prices decoupled from interest rates, cash securities dramatically underperformed synthetic securities (swap contracts designed to mimic cash securities), subordinated bonds at times outperformed senior securities, and so on.

How did all of this contribute to the downfall? For many hedge funds with less complex portfolios—long-short equity, equity market neutral, macro, commodities, etc.—these models would have been an effective part of a broader risk management process. For multi-strategy, credit arbitrage, and other more diverse portfolios, it is possible that the complexity required to generate truly indicative stress tests led to a greater utilization of baseline scenario analysis, which fostered a sense of complacency and led to the assumption of significantly more leverage and risk. Ultimately, against a backdrop of wild volatility, lost financing, underperforming hedges, illiquidity, and other left tail events, this additional risk was just another straw on the back of a camel with very wobbly legs.

Despite these complexities, if a risk manager has the skill, insight, and patience to tailor the model to the particular risks of his or her portfolio, these systems can be an important part of a strong risk management solution. Perhaps they are more akin to a weather vane than Doppler radar, but still they are useful tools in the right hands.

Bitten by the Basis

Once a portfolio or investment is established, the risk model and all of its assumptions effectively set a benchmark for the manager's expectation of performance, in good times and bad. When a manager experiences a significant loss because an investment or its hedge deviates from this theoretical or modeled behavior, the loss tends to be lumped into a giant explanatory bucket referred to as "basis risk." Uncharitably interpreted, this is a technical term for "I underestimated or completely missed the risk inherent in my portfolio and lost a ton of your money as a result."

In the credit crisis of 2008, so many securities diverged from market expectations, and so wildly, that basis risk became an easy catchall for managers wishing to avoid a detailed accounting of their failings. To investors who heard it a few times too often, it became an obscenity. During this crisis, basis risk among previously corre-lated securities was everywhere: subordinated credit outperformed senior credit; synthetic credit (credit default swaps) outperformed cash securities; bonds decoupled from the rate markets; convert-ibles underperformed both high yield and equities; the list went on and on.

In its most extreme and broadly defined form, basis risk naturally played a role in the downfall of nearly every collapsed fund. Manag-ers make assumptions about how the world will behave and express those assumptions in sometimes highly leveraged positions. When reality deviates from that vision, the losses come streaming in.

Sowood: Levered to a Basis Nightmare

As discussed in Chapter 2, Sowood was done in by a confluence of many ill winds. Some were "structural": excessive leverage, illiq-uid positions, and an asset liability duration mismatch, to name a few. But others were purely investment-related. Perhaps the most devastating was a basis risk that emerged between a main invest-ment in the fund and one very critical assumption used in constructing the portfolios hedges. One of the fund's key positions was a highly leveraged investment in senior-secured bank loans. In order to hedge against a decline in the value of these loans, Sowood portfolio managers utilized a short position in high-yield credit and equity puts as hedges against loan price movements. As dis-cussed earlier, they appear to have explicitly assumed that if a downturn appeared in the credit markets, the price of subordinated high-yield debt and equities would decline by more than the price of bank loans—probably around three to five times as much.

Although the basis for such an assumption is generally supported by the historical relationship between loan and high-yield prices, that relationship is an average, a distillation of reality. The relationship between these two assets in different periods has ranged from 1:1 to more than 7:1. Had an investor asked Sowood managers, prior to the collapse, how the fund would perform if loan prices declined 5% (almost unthinkable at the time, but a mere speed bump on the way to a real-world price bottom at approximately 60% of par), chances are that they would have expected a relatively stable performance from the fund. Why? Because their risk model had probably been adjusted to assume high-yield bond prices and equities would decline 15% to 25% if loan prices dropped 5%.

When these embedded "baseline" assumptions were road tested in mid-2007, the results weren't pretty. As loan prices declined by more than 5%, high-yield prices dropped only 5%—effectively a 1:1 ratio. Equity prices declined by even less; as a consequence, Sowood found itself underhedged, overleveraged, and bound for trouble.

Examples like this one illustrate the importance of stress testing each of the price behavior or correlation assumptions embedded in a portfolio. Unfortunately, there was no flashing red light in Sowood's risk model that said, "Danger! If the bank loan market tanks, and your assumption about the price relationship between high yield and bank debt is wrong, you're finished!" Instead, as discussed earlier, the risk models of today require the manager to painstakingly test every possible scenario from the mundane to the highly improbable. With extreme leverage, a realistic analysis should have shown that the margin of error in the hedge performance assumption was very small and that the potential basis risk associated with this investment was exceptionally large. Like smoking at a gas pump, the situation seems harmless enough until suddenly it isn't.

Unfortunately, Sowood is not alone in the annals of basis risk disasters. Many others, like Long-Term Capital Management and Bear Stearns, failed precisely because portfolio managers assumed that the possibility of large price deviations between similar credit instruments, or basis risk, was either very low or zero; therefore no risk management scenario accounted for it, and any hedges that were established to ensure against it were inadequate.

Over the Cliff . . . in a Volkswagen

In the recent history of hedge fund investments, perhaps the most spectacular example of basis risk involved, ironically, one of the most boring companies: Volkswagen. In early 2008, many hedge funds had begun to establish an arbitrage trade that involved purchasing the preferred shares of Volkswagen and short selling the ordinary common shares. By way of background, the ordinary and preferred shares of the company were very similar securities; each represented the same economic ownership in VW, and both paid effectively the same dividend (the preferred shares paid a dividend equal to the ordinary shares, plus a few cents). The main difference between the two shares was the vote—the preferred shares had a lower voting right than the ordinary shares.

In most companies where this difference exists, it accounts for very little in terms of relative valuation. In the case of Volkswagen, however, the preferred shares were trading at a very wide 30% to 40% discount to the value of the ordinary shares. On the surface, this was a hedge fund's dream come true: two similar, relatively liquid shares, trading at a large valuation difference. The frosting on the cake was that Porsche had been buying shares in the company, leading advocates of this trade to believe that Porsche would ultimately buy Volkswagen in its entirety and retire the discounted preferred shares (which the hedge funds were long) at 100% of the value of the ordinaries. This outcome, of course, would produce a big gain for any funds holding these positions as long as the prices of ordinary and preferred shares didn't deviate further before the Porsche acquisition.

But then, in the fall of 2008, with ordinary VW shares trading at approximately 200 euros, something very unexpected happened. When Lehman Brothers filed for bankruptcy, many index funds that had lent their shares to other investors through Lehman (in an effort to make a few extra dollars) lost ownership of the shares completely and were forced to scramble into the market to purchase new ones. This sudden demand caused the price of the ordinary shares to rocket upward, resulting in margin calls to hedge funds that were short the shares. This, in turn, forced many funds to close out both the long and short legs of the trade. To unwind, hedge funds representing hundreds of millions if not billions of dollars were forced to buy back short positions in the ordinary shares and sell the preferreds—all at precisely the same time.

When this process had run its painful course, the ordinary shares (which hedge funds were short) had doubled in value to nearly 400 euros at a time when most automakers' shares had declined by at least 50% due to the slump in the industry. The preferred shares (which hedge funds were long) were crushed, declining by more than 40%.

By hedge fund standards, this was the equivalent of being disemboweled. But it wasn't over. Porsche later announced that it intended to grow its stake in the company to as much as 75%.[1] Investors quickly realized that the combination of the increased Porsche stake and the German state of Lower Saxony's existing stake left only ~5% of the outstanding shares available for purchase to cover a short position. The result: panic. Anyone still in the trade had to buy, sending Volkswagen common shares up another 250% to nearly 1,000 euros. At this point, the preferred shares had declined to a value of roughly *5% of the ordinaries*—completely crushing any remaining investors. Thus ended one of the most extraordinary examples of basis risk ever recorded. A graph of the bloodshed appears in Figure 3-1.

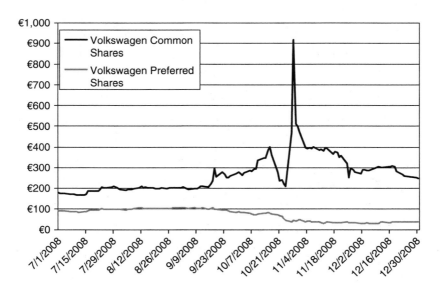

Figure 3-1 Price of Volkswagen common vs. preferred shares
Source: Bloomberg

Many hedge funds reported losing monumental sums of money, some as much as $500 million on this single arbitrage trade and variations on the same theme. Had you visited the offices of these hedge funds in the summer of 2007, you might have heard a portfolio manager describing the compelling returns this opportunity offered. But the risk associated with the trade? They likely would have argued that the downside was limited since the trade was "dollar neutral" (equally long and short), "well hedged," and short duration (given the Porsche involvement).

Theoretically, they'd have been correct. The investment was designed to have very little downside risk by being short an ordinary share against a nearly identical preferred share. Any risk model that stress tested this investment within a broader portfolio would have simply assumed that any increase or decrease in the preferred shares would have been equally matched by an offsetting gain or loss in the ordinaries. And yet things did go terribly wrong, reminding participants that the potential for basis risk in hedged positions can be limitless.

Everything That Can Go Wrong . . .

Up to this point, this chapter has examined examples of basis risk involving similar securities: senior versus subordinated debt in the Sowood debacle, and ordinary versus preferred shares in the Volkswagen mishap. In 2008, basis risk preyed on nearly identical securities as well. It was, at the time, an equal opportunity destroyer of value in hedge funds.

The relationship in early 2008 between the "cash" bank loan market and the Loan Credit Default Swap Index (LCDX) provides one such example. The LCDX is a tradable derivative bank loan index that represents 100 credit default swaps referencing the largest most recently issued loans and is thereby designed to be a strong proxy for the overall loan market. Many multi-strategy or credit hedge funds that carry loan exposure have sought to utilize the LCDX as a hedge. Given the significant overlap between the assets underlying the LCDX and the cash bank loan market, most market players assumed that the prices of the two instruments would trade with a correlation of near one and that any basis risk between the two would be both small and short-lived.

These expectations, like many others at the time, were soon shattered. Between March and April 2008, the spread between the prices of cash bank loans and the LCDX—two instruments that effectively referenced the same asset—widened to a level previously unseen, a price difference of approximately 9%. Anyone who was long bank loans in early March and hedged with LCDX was, by the end of April, on his way to the proverbial woodshed. Over this period, the cash loan market rose from 88% to 89% (a $10 million gain on a $1 billion loan portfolio), and the LCDX rose approximately six points, to nearly 98% (a loss of $60 million on a $1 billion hedge); together, this produced a $50 million loss on a "totally hedged" portfolio. If a hedge fund manager was unfortunate enough to have utilized three times leverage, that loss would have amounted to $150 million. Before this price deviation occurred, very few managers would have even considered a divergence of this magnitude a possible risk, let alone account for it in any risk analysis or portfolio hedge. In fact, this is the type of risk that no risk model will highlight. Even the most sophisticated hedge fund risk managers would disregard it due to the relative implausibility of its occurrence.

Interestingly, this arguably anomalous price deviation had very little to do with the fundamentals of the bank loan market. Instead, it was driven by relatively unpredictable technical factors. In particular, as the credit crisis was burgeoning, financing for cash bank loan investments had effectively dried up for all but the most established hedge fund managers. Without any leverage, the net (after 2% and 20% fees), all-in (including any discount to par) return of most noninvestment-grade bank loans was less than 10% — hardly an attractive figure to potential investors.

The LCDX is structured as a swap and therefore has leverage effectively built in. As a result, many funds that were looking for a leveraged, easily tradable, long exposure to the loan market turned to the LCDX contracts. This, combined with the ongoing unwind of LCDX hedges from liquidating loan portfolios, caused a technically driven price surge well in excess of the underlying cash loan market that simply couldn't be matched or arbitraged away. For the remaining hedge funds still managing long portfolios of bank loans and using the LCDX to hedge, this was yet another blow.

As 2008 wore on, examples of basis risk continued to sprout like weeds in the most unexpected places, contributing to the growing realization that no price relationship assumption, no matter how fundamentally valid or theoretically intuitive, could be relied upon in a highly stressed market. The only real hedge during this period was fewer positions.

Modeling in Liquidity Nirvana

So far, this chapter has focused on some of the inherent shortcomings of theoretical risk modeling: hedge effectiveness assumptions; analyzing the impact of risk of one market while assuming the rest of the world is calm; systematic underappreciation of basis risk, and others. Unfortunately, the challenge of translating risk model sensitivity runs into real-world predictive analysis doesn't end there. In fact, most risk models completely omit one of the most significant risk factors in any portfolio: liquidity. The baseline assumption embedded in most risk models is that all securities in a portfolio are infinitely liquid at the current market price. As nearly every hedge fund that lived (or died) during the credit crisis of 2008 can now attest, this assumption is deeply flawed. In that tempest, market liquidity for many securities or asset classes experienced steep declines or ceased to exist altogether, exacerbating losses in funds that were trying to de-lever and accelerating the demise of many others, including Sowood and Bear Stearns.

Without a realistic assumption regarding liquidity, it is also easy for a risk model to ignore the impact of unstable debt and equity capital within the fund. Think about it. If you assume that every security is supremely liquid, it doesn't matter if your fund loses all of its debt financing and equity capital tomorrow; the fund can simply sell all of its positions at last sale by lunchtime the same day. If only the world were this kind.

Fortunately, the long, bruising road of misguided scenario analysis, flawed hedge assumptions, leverage multipliers, illiquidity, and many ifs, buts, and maybes has provided the hedge fund industry with a number of valuable lessons. Probably at the top of this list is the importance of establishing an effective risk management process. Here the framework is clear: It requires a highly integrated and collaborative effort involving an exceptionally skilled risk management team, deeply involved senior investment officers, and an operations arm that can establish and monitor a capital base that matches the duration of the fund's assets. It further requires risk limits and ample excess cash sufficient to weather unexpected volatility in asset prices, ineffective hedges, periods of illiquidity, and variations in equity capital. That's a long list, but with the amount of money the funds are entrusted with, will anything less do?

four

HEDGE FUND CORRELATION

At its peak in mid-2008, the total amount of capital managed by the hedge fund industry stood at an estimated $2.9 trillion. As noted in Chapter 2, this figure was nowhere near the total amount of hedge fund investments in the market at that time. Before the credit crisis hit in late 2008, a conservative estimate of leverage use in the industry would have been around 2.5 times the base number (total long investments divided by capital under management), which suggests that hedge funds controlled more than $7 trillion of long investments. And, by definition, these were "hedged" funds, so it's fair to assume that they controlled, on average, a similar number of short positions. The combined total may have approached $14 trillion of long and short investments, more than the current gross domestic product of the United States.

The sheer magnitude of these numbers raises a very interesting question: with so much capital chasing a presumably limited pool of "mispriced," and thus attractive, assets, how do hedge funds find unique investments? In many strategies, like convertible arbitrage, risk arbitrage, equity event-driven, and others, the answer is: they really don't. They end up owning similarly constructed portfolios filled with overlapping pools of the same assets. And given the total amount of leveraged capital they can deploy, they can end up controlling the vast majority of the entire outstanding opportunity set in certain strategies.

Consider the market for convertible arbitrage. According to industry estimates, the total par value of U.S. dollar denominated convertible bonds outstanding is approximately $300 billion. Of this amount, hedge fund managers appear to control at least 70% to 80%, with the rest left to mutual funds like Fidelity or other long oriented investors. As you might have guessed, hedge fund dominance of this asset class is achieved largely through borrowed money.

In early 2008, an estimated $75 billion of hedge fund assets were focused on convertible arbitrage. On average, this capital was leveraged at least three times, allowing the managers to collectively control long assets of $225 billion or more. Not surprisingly, ownership of this $225 billion appears to be very narrowly held, mirroring the concentration of assets under management in the broader hedge fund industry.

In Table 4-1, the top ten holders of three of the largest benchmark convertible bonds outstanding are highlighted. Shown in italic, hedge funds dominate the ownership of each bond, controlling between 65% and 100% of each list.

This data reveals a number of "300-pound gorillas" roaming the convertible clubhouse. With a combined total of $40 billion or more under management, Citadel, Aristeia, Lydian, and Highbridge

Table 4-1 Top Holders of Selected Large Convertible Bonds as of December 31, 2008

Ford Motor Company	Advanced Micro Devices	Micron Technology
4.25% Convertible Bonds of 2036	6% Convertible Bonds of 2015	1.875% Convertible Bonds of 2014
Amount Outstanding: $4.95BB	*Amount Outstanding: $2.1BB*	*Amount Outstanding: $1.3BB*

Holder	Amount Held ($MM)	Holder	Amount Held ($MM)	Holder	Amount Held ($MM)
Citigroup	*751,019*	Fidelity Management	196,609	*Citadel Inv Group*	*231,571*
Citadel Inv Group	*466,006*	Citigroup	167,528	*Aristeia Capital*	*136,200*
Aristeia Capital	*428,100*	Och-Ziff Capital Mgmt.	117,500	*Lydian Asset Mgmt.*	*135,500*
Bank of America	*357,948*	Capital World Inv.	111,015	*UBS O'Connor*	*78,000*
Whitebox Advisors	*268,806*	Citadel Inv. Group	92,500	*Highbridge Capital Mgmt.*	*67,167*
Polygon Investment	*205,000*	Capital Research	92,245	*Camden Asset*	*38,250*
APG All Pensions Group	163,500	Lydian Asset Mgmt.	84,000	*Citigroup*	*34,036*
Deutsche Bank AG	*148,911*	Whitebox Advisors	82,276	*DE Shaw & Co*	*32,500*
T Rowe Price	143,346	*Aristeia Capital*	68,246	*Zazove Assoc.*	*30,000*
Highbridge Capital Mgmt	*122,677*	Waterstone Asset Mgmt.	58,150	*Merrill Lynch & Co.*	*28,589*
Top Ten Holders	3,055,313	Top Ten Holders	1,070,069	Top Ten Holders	811,813

Source: 13F filings, Bloomberg.

alone can dominate the ownership of many bonds in the market—and they do.

Interestingly, Table 4-1 also reveals the presence of Citigroup and other banks in the market. At least part of these holdings represent convertibles that the banks hold on "swap" for their clients. This is an arrangement where a bank provides leverage to a hedge fund by entering into a swap agreement in which the bank pays the total return of the convertible bond to the hedge fund, and the hedge fund pays a modest, fixed rate of interest. The amount of leverage provided to the hedge fund is equal to the difference between the market value of the bond and the amount of cash collateral (the "haircut") that the hedge fund must post against the swap.

The banks hold the actual bonds as a hedge against their obligations under the swap and therefore appear in the 13F ownership filings (SEC quarterly security holding reports). Given the prevalence of these arrangements, bank holdings are often hedge funds in disguise, and they will behave as such whenever a crisis arises.

The Gazelle Factor

So what does it matter to individual investors if strategies like convertible bonds are dominated by hedge funds? For an investor in a convertible hedge fund, the answer is simple: this type of concentrated ownership significantly magnifies the downside risk. When a single type of investor owns 70% of an entire asset class, any stress that affects one investor tends to have a similar effect on all investors, like a lion approaching a herd of gazelle. And as you might imagine, in the convertible market, as in other markets, there is no shortage of systemic events, market crises, and other vulnerabilities that can periodically touch off a chaotic stampede among the gazelle.

The first of these vulnerabilities is leverage. As discussed earlier, in convertible arbitrage, most managers pursue a strategy that involves buying convertible bonds with leverage and then selling short common stock of the issuer against the bond as a hedge. In addition, some managers will also attempt to purchase credit default swaps (credit insurance) against the convertible to protect against deterioration in the credit quality of the bond. Together, these hedges provide the theoretical support for leverage in the strategy: by lowering the expected volatility of the investment, they create a more consistent and therefore leverageable return profile. With this in mind, both banks and hedge funds have historically justified the use of leverage at levels between roughly three and ten times the amount of capital underlying each convertible bond.

This level of leverage poses a more systemic risk for hedge funds that goes far beyond the obvious risk associated with utilizing leverage in any individual investment. This risk stems from the basic duration of convertible bonds and the facilities hedge fund managers use to leverage them. Most convertible bonds have a lifespan of 2 to 10 years, yet they are almost always financed with overnight or other short-term prime brokerage borrowings. Furthermore, many managers rely on equity capital that is rarely locked up for more than 90 days. In normal market conditions, this isn't a problem; given the large number of hedge funds that play in the space, the average daily trading volume in convertible securities can usually absorb a liquidation of one fund or a small group of funds without impacting broader market levels or the behavior of other hedge funds.

However, when an event causes a much broader, marketwide loss of hedge fund debt or equity capital, the façade of market liquidity can quickly evaporate. In the face of heavy hedge fund selling and few natural buyers, the market becomes increasingly one-sided, bid-offer spreads widen, and trading activity dries up. Of course, for many funds, this loss of market liquidity comes at precisely the wrong time, just when their loss of debt of equity capital is forcing them to sell. With few options, many funds have no choice but to sell at deeply discounted prices.

The events that can cause this abrupt loss of hedge fund capital are not that hard to imagine: sharply negative or sustained poor investment performance, a pullback of bank lending to the space, a change in the regulatory framework for the strategy, etc. When these events happen, they also tend to inflict a disproportionate amount of pain on the largest players in the market, which inevitably produces a rash of herd-spooking rumors that involve the demise of one or more of the 300-pound gorillas.

Together, this sequence of events—unstable capital structures, widespread loss of capital, heavy selling, illiquid markets, and stressed asset sales—forms the basis of "hedge fund correlation" risk. The events of the second half of 2008 illustrate the potentially dire consequences of this phenomenon.

The Perfect Storm

With the credit crisis worsening in the fall of 2008, banks found it increasingly difficult to raise capital in the interbank market. As liquidity dried up, the Federal Reserve was forced to intervene and fund the banks with short-term capital.

Under the terms of these funding agreements, the Fed listed pre-approved, on balance sheet, fixed income securities that the banks could use as collateral to secure the borrowings. Unfortunately for many hedge funds, convertible securities were not included; once banks were unable to borrow against convertibles, their interest in financing them started to wane. (Remember, many banks provide leverage to hedge funds through a swap transaction. In this structure, the bank holds the actual bond on its balance sheet, which it hopes to then releverage.) As the crisis deepened, banks and prime brokers began a systematic process of either significantly reducing financing for convertibles or pulling it altogether.

While no official data exists on how much liquidity was removed from the market, it appears that between September and November 2008, the amount of outstanding convertible financing was reduced by at least two-thirds; what remained became substantially more expensive to hold.

The process employed by the banks to achieve such a rapid deflation of the convertible balloon is probably best described as blunt force trauma—all stick and no carrot. As explained in Chapter 2, most of the terms involved in prime broker financing—including levels for leverage, financing cost, and other terms for each class of securities—are contractually fixed for a predetermined period of time. For many larger, more established funds in the convertible market, this period is a one- to three-month "rolling" term, provided the fund maintains its margin requirements and doesn't breach any other important covenants. If the prime broker calls "term" at any time, it means that the fund, at the end of a one- to three-month "term-out" period, must either accept any changes the prime broker is proposing to the financing or, if the financing facility is being terminated, return the capital. As you might imagine, the term-out period is important to many funds because it gives them time to find a potential replacement for the current facility.

In late 2008, many prime brokers and banks apparently decided this documented contractual process was too cumbersome and time consuming in the midst of a growing crisis. In the absence of any apparent breach of contractual covenants, some prime brokers reportedly just ignored the agreements and began to dramatically reduce leverage allocated to convertible hedge funds, if they didn't pull the financing altogether. For the most part, this was accomplished by unilaterally raising the minimum collateral requirements for a hedged convertible security from the stated contractual level—for example, 10% (10 times leverage)—to somewhere in the neighborhood of 40% (2.5 times leverage) or more. Any financing that remained was subjected to a unilateral increase in cost, jumping from fed funds plus ~25 bps (2.25%) to somewhere about LIBOR plus 300 (4.5%).

As mentioned earlier, most funds had little choice but to accept these new terms. In the middle of the worst financial crisis in a generation, turning to another broker (who would just offer similar terms) or suing to enforce the original contract was impractical.

The bad news traveled fast. In a strategy where 60% to 80% of the capital supporting the investments is leverage, reports of that resource being pulled systematically were like shouts of "fire" in a crowded theater. If you hadn't gotten the call regarding leverage from your prime broker, you knew it was coming. Hedge funds had no choice but to sell positions and sell them fast. As they did, liquidity became increasingly scarce and bid-offer spreads began to widen.

As these forces gathered steam in mid-September, events began to unfold that would add the equivalent of rocket fuel to an already intense fire. The first of these was the Lehman Brothers bankruptcy. As a prime broker for many hedge funds, Lehman's demise made orphans of many that had tapped it for leverage. Some of the funds found new homes for their positions but usually at far less favorable terms. Many others were left homeless. Regardless of which group a fund fell into, the outcome was the same: it sold securities to reduce leverage. Furthermore, Lehman reportedly had had a big proprietary desk. For the convertibles in that portfolio, the answer was the same: sell. More fuel for the fire.

The second negative catalyst was the near-global ban on short selling of financial services companies that was enacted after Lehman's fall. Most convertible hedge funds short shares of the underlying company in order to hedge a convertible investment. For many, with no way to hedge, the short sale ban meant that they had to sell many financial convertibles in their portfolios. With financial service companies representing approximately 20% of the convertible market, this ruling fanned the flames even more.

If all this trouble wasn't enough to make a convertible arbitrage manager sell, the rumors that started swirling around the campfire in October probably were. Citadel Investment Group, a fund with roughly $16 billion under management—a convertible market gorilla to be sure—supposedly was in trouble.[1] The whispers got so loud that its management held a conference call in an attempt to quell the speculation. Founder Ken Griffin and Chief Operating Officer Gerald Beeson confirmed that Citadel had suffered losses of 35% year-to-date in its two core funds, Kensington and

Wellington. But they also argued that limited redemptions, $8 billion in undrawn credit lines, and cash equal to 30% of capital provided cause for continued faith in the funds. "We have made it through 18 years . . . and we will make it through the next six to eight weeks."[2]

That such reassurance was even necessary seemed to portend more trouble, to say nothing of Citadel's enormous losses. No convertible investor could have taken heart in the description of current market conditions, from the same conference call: "To call it a dislocation doesn't go anywhere near what we've seen. We've seen a near collapse of the world's banking system."

At its peak, Citadel reportedly managed approximately $20 billion. Given the fund's history of leverage use (an SEC filing in 2006 placed the fund's leverage at 7.8 to 1), the market would have assumed that the fund had long investments totaling between at least $60 and $120 billion. Although not all of this would have been invested in convertibles, Citadel had a history as a major player in that market. Table 4-1 shows that Citadel had a total of nearly $800 million invested in three bonds alone. However one did the math, it was clear that billions of dollars of convertible positions would be forced onto the market if Citadel alone lost its capital.

And if that wasn't enough, many hedge fund investors were unhappy with the negative absolute returns being posted by hedge funds, which raised the threat of equity capital redemptions. Since most hedge funds require investors to provide 60 days notice of any redemption requests, year-end demands for capital were being delivered in the weeks leading up to November 1. Yet another reason to sell positions.

In March 2009, *Absolute Return* magazine reported that Citadel's AUM had declined from $20 billion in 2008 to $12 billion in January 2009. Given the highly negative market tone in the second half of the year, assume that 75% of this $8 billion loss occurred in the third and fourth quarters of 2008. If *Absolute Return's* numbers are correct and one further assumes that Citadel wanted to maintain leverage of five times its AUM throughout this period, then it would have had to either sell close to $30 billion of securities over the course of a few months or significantly raise its leverage—both very difficult tasks at the time.

As other convertible players calculated the impact of these issues on the market, nearly all reacted in kind: sell first, ask questions later. Given all of the systemic factors at play—loss of bank capital, Lehman, the short sale rule, stress among the largest players, the impending loss of equity capital—who could blame them? Convertible managers inherently understood that the liquidity in the market was (and is) only a function of two-way interest from hedge funds. Once the market becomes all supply and no demand, there is only one question: who gets out first, and who is left holding the bag?

The Impact

The key to this series of unfortunate events in the convertible market is that each one required hedge fund managers to sell positions. Whether dealing with the loss of bank financing, equity capital, a prime broker, or critical hedging capabilities, hedge fund managers had no choice but to unload positions and to do it all at roughly the same time. Why? Because three-quarters of the market's participants pursued the same arbitrage strategy, with a similar amount of leverage, financed by the same banks, supported by equity capital raised largely from the same group of investors.

Demonstrating hedge fund correlation in the credit crisis is the easy part. The greater challenge lies in quantifying the impact of that correlation on the performance of convertible hedge funds. Unfortunately, there is no easy way to accomplish this. A reasonable starting point would be to compare the performance of convertible hedge funds with funds less susceptible to the correlation problem. Figure 4-1 compares the performance of the Dow Jones Convertible Arbitrage Hedge Fund Index (an index of the actual, net of fee returns generated by a group of convertible arbitrage hedge funds) to the Dow Jones Equity Long/Short Hedge Fund Index (a similar index focused on long-short hedge fund managers).

With a global market capitalization of publicly traded stocks totaling roughly $40 trillion—including $8 trillion in the United States—the market for long-short equity opportunities is substantially less crowded, generally less leveraged by the manager, and therefore less prone to hedge fund correlation risk.

As shown in Figure 4-1, the return profiles of these two strategies were not dramatically different until the fall of 2008. From that point forward, convertible arbitrage as a strategy began to underperform drastically, ending 2008 down nearly 50%—over 30% worse than long-short equity. Remember that both of these strategies are, by definition, hedged with shares of common stock. The main difference is the long positions in each strategy. Convertible arbitrage is long a convertible bond and short common stock. Long-short equity is long one share of common stock and short another.

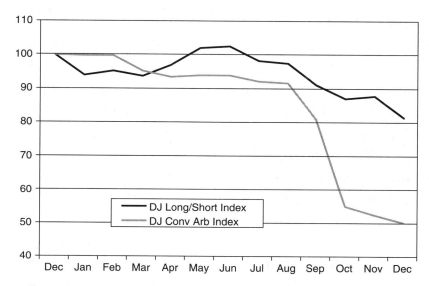

Figure 4-1 The Dow Jones Equity Long/Short Hedge Fund Index vs. the Dow Jones Convertible Arbitrage Hedge Fund Index (indexed to 100%, December 31, 2007)
Source: Dow Jones Hedge Fund Indexes, Inc.

Together, these facts point to hedge fund correlation as a major factor behind the dramatic underperformance of convertible arbitrage during this period. One might argue, however, that convertible hedge funds underperformed because they used more leverage than long-short funds. While this may be true, the strategy required it to produce competitive returns. Furthermore, the security that was being leveraged was a bond, which should have provided more protection than the long equity leg of a long-short strategy during the downturn in the market. However you slice it, convertible arbitrage was one of the worst performing hedge fund strategies for 2008 and a particularly painful place for investors in search of "absolute returns."

The GM Fiasco

While the convertible arbitrage wipeout of 2008 was arguably the most extreme case of hedge fund correlation, it was not the first time it had occurred. In May 2005, Standard & Poor's downgrade of General Motors, from investment to noninvestment grade, was the catalyst for a similar episode. At that time, GM had several billion dollars of convertible bonds outstanding, making it one of the most widely held bellwether issuers in the market. True to form, most convertible arbitrage investors holding GM bonds were positioned long the convertible and short GM stock.

Normally, a simple downgrade of a company does not incite mayhem in the convertible market. This situation was different for two reasons. First, the downgrade was not a normal one; with a noninvestment grade, junk rating, GM bonds could no longer be held by certain, investment grade–only managers, such as pension funds. Second, junk status meant that GM bonds had to be dropped from certain key investment grade indexes. It all added up to outsized pressure on the price of GM credit.

The Kerkorian Dagger

When a company's credit is deteriorating, convertible investors generally assume that its stock price will decline in sympathy with the bond market. If this assumption proves correct, the gains generated by the short stock leg of the convertible arbitrage investment can help offset any losses suffered in the convertible bond portion of the trade. Tragically, this was not the case with the GM downgrade.

At about the same time that Standard & Poor's passed its judgment, Kirk Kerkorian launched a plan to purchase 28 million shares of the company's stock at a premium to the current market price, which sent the stock soaring 15%. For convertible arbitrage investors, either occurrence would have caused severe pain; together, they made for a Chernobyl scenario. Hedge funds were hit first by a significant rating downgrade on a leveraged long position and then, instead of getting help from the hedge, they got punched again by a bid for the company's shares, which caused the short stock position to rise and hemorrhage more cash. It was an extreme case of basis risk, causing significant losses on all legs of the investment.

Just as would be the case more than three years later, rumors of major losses were rampant in 2005. The *New York Times* reported rumors of severe declines at Highbridge Capital Management, which managed approximately $7 billion, and at GLG Partners, a London-based firm owned by Lehman. Not to be left out, banks were said to be sustaining major losses through exposure to hedge funds invested in GM bonds.[3]

It still isn't clear how accurate these reports were. Some funds, including Highbridge, went out of their way to quell the rumors, even sending letters to investors that denied the losses. What is certain is that convertible investors lost a significant amount of money as a result of this event. These losses, coupled with the fear of failure and potential liquidation at other funds, contributed to another round of "hedge fund correlation"–driven selling in the strategy. According to the Dow Jones hedge fund indexes, convertible arbitrage investors lost 7.34% in the three months ending May 2005. For the full year, convertible arbitrage recorded the worst performance (by more than 733 basis points) of all hedge fund strategies that Dow Jones tracks.

SEC Chairman William Donaldson offered prescient commentary on the episode and the overall danger of hedge fund correlation.

> Every week seems to bring another article in the press about the crowding of hedge funds into similar investment strategies and the difficulty that this implies for hedge fund managers eager to post market-beating returns. If history is any guide, it is just this sort of pressure that can lead otherwise well-intentioned professionals to pursue practices that can ultimately result in disaster for the investors they serve.[4]

Indeed.

Picking Up Nickels in Front of a Bulldozer

In addition to convertible arbitrage, a number of other asset classes tend to be dominated by hedge funds and therefore contribute to the hedge fund correlation problem.

Risk arbitrage, another hedge fund magnet, is high on the list. Risk arbitrage is a strategy that seeks to capture the difference between the offered purchase price and the current market price of stock in a company that is the subject of a takeover or merger offer. The difference between these two prices, for deals that the market expects will be completed, is usually between 3% and 10%. And given that most merger and acquisition transactions are completed in three or four months, the annualized return for a risk arbitrage investment can easily be in the double digits. Many long-only institutional stock managers, having realized close to 95% of the fair value of their investment upon the announcement of a takeover, have no interest in owning the shares for the final few months. This is precisely when hedge funds *do* want to own the shares. In a stock-for-stock merger transaction, where investors in the target company receive shares of the acquirer, hedge funds purchase shares of the target company, typically at a discount of several percentage points below the announced takeover price, and then short sell the shares of the acquiring company as a hedge.

If the acquiring company is paying cash for the target company's shares, most hedge funds either buy and hold the target shares unhedged or try to establish a basket hedge of other industry names. Either way, if the transaction closes as expected, the returns (enhanced by some leverage, of course) can be attractive. But if the merger falls apart, the shares of the target company can plunge and create major losses for the hedge funds. A pattern of consistent, modest monthly gains punctuated by the occasional catastrophic loss has led to risk arbitrage being described as "picking up nickels in front of a bulldozer."

Because the strategy is dominated by hedge funds and, as with convertible arbitrage, all of the funds tend to carry similar deals, when the bulldozer runs over one hedge fund, it runs over most of the rest. When one risk arbitrage deal "breaks," it tends to create a need for funds to sell other merger arbitrage stocks to reduce leverage, which, in turn, pressures returns at all funds involved in the strategy. Hedge fund correlation strikes again.

The Three Horsemen of Hedge Fund Correlation

The potential for hedge fund correlation risk exists wherever three key conditions are met:

1. The total size of an asset class is limited to an amount that hedge funds alone can dominate (usually less than $500 billion).
2. Significant leverage is necessary to implement the strategy.
3. Structural implementation of the strategy is largely uniform from one investor to another.

Other strategies that share some of these correlation-causing characteristics to various degrees include capital structure and other credit arbitrage strategies, distressed, event-driven, and certain quantitative strategies.

Many strategies do manage to hide from the horsemen. They often operate in markets that are too large for any one group to dominate and involve investments that vary from investor to investor. As mentioned earlier, long-short equity is certainly one example. There will always be certain long-short magnet stocks, but the multitrillion-dollar size of the equity markets tends to prevent bouts of deep systemic damage in this strategy. Similarly, certain global macro and commodity focused strategies—which target very deep and liquid markets—are also less prone to hedge fund correlation risk.

Overall, investments in hedge fund strategies that carry correlation risk are more likely to experience deeper drawdowns and more frequent losses of underlying investment liquidity than other strategies. Arguably, investors who are willing to bear this additional risk should also demand higher returns over time. If the strategies fail to provide greater returns for assuming correlation risk, capital should naturally flow away from the strategy until the risk-return profile improves.

five

THE HEDGE FUND
PETER PRINCIPLE

N amed for its creator, Dr. Lawrence J. Peter, the Peter Principle hypothesizes that employees in a corporate hierarchy tend to rise through an organization until they exceed their personal level of competence. In other words, people get promoted in their jobs until they reach a position that is beyond their personal capabilities, and once they attain this position, they remain there, creating an ineffective and potentially dysfunctional organization.

As AUM skyrocketed in the hedge fund industry, a very similar phenomenon seems to have developed. In the hedge fund version, however, the Peter Principle applies not to employees but to the funds themselves, and its consequences threaten fund performance, risk management, and, in some cases, the very survival of the hedge fund itself.

This problem tends to begin when a fund, experiencing rapid growth in AUM, starts to exhaust opportunities in its original core competency. To sustain its growth, the fund begins to seek new opportunities in less familiar strategies or asset classes. As the fund moves further and further from its core area of expertise, the potential for poor performance and inadequate risk management increases.

The progression of such a fund typically begins with a talented manager who starts out with one or two focused core investment strategies. Over time, with a little skill and good fortune, the fund generates an attractive return on capital for its investors. Satisfied investors then eagerly commit more capital, and the fund grows in both assets and personnel.

This process continues year after year until the fund's capital base grows too large to commit solely to its original strategy. At this point, the fund risks becoming a 300-pound gorilla in the marketplace. As the largest holder of many of its positions, its risk has become increasingly concentrated, and it faces less and less liquidity in many of its key investments.

In an effort to sidestep these annoying roadblocks to even greater personal wealth, the manager then begins to shift away from the fund's core strategy or strategies and looks to "bolt on" fresh investment teams who will pursue new strategies. This evolution continues until the fund wanders far enough away from its core investment expertise that it begins to make investments and assume risk in markets where it lacks the necessary investment expertise, or, if it does have the talent, lacks management experience to competently assess and control the risks the portfolio managers are taking. As the fund's risk oversight weakens, the volatility of its returns increases significantly, leading to a substantially greater chance of catastrophic loss.

Interestingly, fund documents don't merely permit each of these developments; they encourage them. Most funds grant the manager broad discretion to choose among a wide array of strategies; to select from a nearly unlimited menu of securities, derivatives, private investments, and other assets; to choose where, geographically, to deploy the capital; and to determine how much leverage the fund will use to supercharge whatever it ends up owning.

In effect, investors simply trust that the manager will not permit significant "style drift." Otherwise, it is up to the investors to exercise their right to redeem their capital from the manager. Unfortunately, when changes in investment strategy set the Peter Principle in motion, it's rare that any warning bell starts ringing. Only a diligent hedge fund investor, with deep knowledge of the background and skill of the fund's management team and a wary eye surveying the allocation of capital, will be able to see an approaching cliff before the car drives over it.

The Amaranth Meltdown

Amaranth Advisors, a defunct, multibillion-dollar hedge fund, was one possible victim of the Peter Principle. Nicholas Maounis founded Amaranth in 2000 with approximately $600 million. Prior to forming Amaranth, he was a portfolio manager at another multi-strategy hedge fund, Paloma Partners, which specialized primarily in convertible and other arbitrage strategies. While at Paloma, Maounis developed a reputation as a particularly talented convertible trader, earning the respect of the fund's senior management and others in the marketplace. When he decided to leave Paloma, Maounis initially sought to caste Amaranth in the same multi-strategy mold as Paloma, with a focus on convertible and other arbitrage strategies. Further strengthening the connection, he took with him more than 20 of Paloma's portfolio managers, analysts, and other professionals.[1] Despite the talent drain, Paloma was supportive, sharing its back office and committing an investment to the new fund.[2]

In its first few years of operation, Amaranth generated particularly attractive returns for investors, totaling approximately 29%, 15%, and 21% in 2001, 2002, and 2003, respectively.[3] Not surprisingly, as its record of successful performance grew, the fund attracted billions of dollars in new investor capital.

As 2004 unfolded, however, the performance of its core convertible arbitrage strategy had become less exciting than in previous years, limiting the fund's total return to just 3% net of fees by the third quarter.[4] At this point, the fund faced two key challenges in its convertible business: new issue volumes in the market, which tend to be a significant source of hedge profit, were at their lowest level since the late 1990s, and market volatility, the life blood of arbitrage trading profits, was near its lowest level in a decade. With the outlook for the fund's core investment strategy less certain, the prospects for significant additional asset growth were probably diminishing as well.

During this period of low returns, the fund began to shift a portion of its capital away from convertible and other traditional forms of arbitrage and into energy trading. Although Amaranth had first expanded into energy strategies in 2002 with the addition of several former Enron traders, energy trading represented a fraction of its portfolio until 2005.

The man ultimately entrusted to lead this expansion into energy trading was a 32-year-old Canadian trader named Brian Hunter. Hunter was hired in mid-2004 from Deutsche Bank and promoted to cohead of the firm's commodities group in 2005. For Hunter, the timing of his arrival couldn't have been better. With returns in its core strategies suffering, Amaranth was undoubtedly searching for something new to fill its P&L void and continue driving the growth of its multibillion-dollar capital pool.

Hunter wasted no time pushing open this door. After a series successful trades, he was allowed to charge ahead, growing Amaranth's exposure to energy arbitrage from a few percentage points to approximately 30% of the fund's assets by mid-2005.[5] With billions of dollars now at his disposal, Hunter set a bold course, betting much of the firm's capital on a variety of highly leveraged, arcane arbitrage strategies in which he assumed big risks in exchange for big potential returns. Although he pursued investments involving a wide array of securities and commodity types, the majority of the capital he deployed was concentrated in a few core strategies.

One of the first—and most aggressive—involved buying deep out-of-the-money call options on natural gas. Given the inherent leverage in options, these trades provided the fund with an opportunity to profit handsomely from any price spikes that might occur over time.

Despite the growing size of the fund's energy positions, the first six months of 2005 proved to be relatively quiet, with a net return of approximately −1%. By fall, however, one of Hunter's exceptionally large out-of-the-money call option bets on natural gas had paid off—in a big way. As Hurricanes Katrina and Rita ripped through the Gulf of Mexico, natural gas and oil production were severely impacted, which led to dramatic price spikes across many

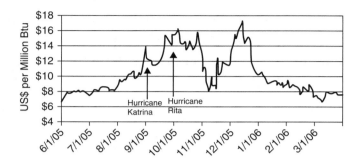

Figure 5-1 Natural gas prices, 2005 to 2006
Source: Bloomberg

different commodities. The rise in natural gas was so sharp that these call options and other natural gas investments generated a profit that would account for the majority of the fund's 21% gain for the full year.[6] See Figure 5-1.

Whether the bet succeeded due to luck or skill was irrelevant. What mattered most was that the fund's performance was back on track, and the prospects for further capital growth were once again bright. The impact of these bets on the fund's performance is highlighted in Table 5-1.

Table 5-1 Amaranth Returns, 2005

Month	Monthly Returns	Year-to-Date Return
June 2005	3.03%	−0.98%
July 2005	2.39%	1.38%
August 2005	5.19%	6.65%
September 2005	7.49%	14.63%
October 2005	−0.90%	13.60%
November 2005	3.48%	17.53%
December 2005	3.13%	21.21%

Source: Excessive Speculation in the Natural Gas Market, United States Senate Permanent Subcommittee on Investigations, June 25, 2007

With this success came staggering personal financial rewards for the fund's principals. In 2005, Hunter reportedly walked away with more than $75 million.[7] For his efforts, Maounis apparently received more than $70 million[8]—good money in Greenwich, Connecticut, exceptionally good money in Alberta, Canada, where Hunter was based. After receiving this lottery-like payout, Hunter could be seen cruising the streets of Calgary in both a Ferrari F430 Spider and a Bentley Arnage (apparently, the Bentley was better suited to the town's snowy winter driving conditions).[9]

With yet another successful yearly performance under its belt, the fund's AUM continued to grow, reaching approximately $8 billion by early 2006. It employed more than 400 people around the globe in six separate offices (Greenwich, London, Toronto, Singapore, Calgary, and Houston). Its team included a remarkably large risk management group staffed by a chief risk officer and 12 risk lieutenants.

Armed with billions more in capital and an air of invincibility, Amaranth entered 2006 intent on wagering dramatically more capital in the energy markets. The trade that would now take center stage comprised investments in a series of natural gas "calendar spreads," which involve trading the difference in price between two contracts for the future delivery of natural gas in different calendar months.

As with any commodity, natural gas futures contracts tend to be driven by the fundamentals of production, inventory, and consumption. For natural gas in particular, the price to purchase the commodity in future months has always had a significant seasonality to it: prices are higher in winter months, when consumer demand for natural gas for home heating is high, and lower in the summer,

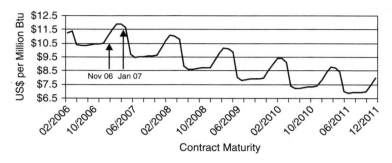

Figure 5-2 NYMEX natural gas forward curve, December 2005
Source: Bloomberg

when demand wanes. Figure 5-2 shows the forward price curve to purchase natural gas on the New York Mercantile Exchange (NYMEX) as of December 2005.

As highlighted in the graph, prices for delivery of natural gas in the summer months tend to be $1 to $2 lower than contracts to purchase in the winter months. Furthermore, the longer-term trend for gas prices was generally lower at that time on expectations that growing supplies would outpace demand for the commodity.

For Amaranth, this forward price curve represented a ripe opportunity to trade the price fluctuations from one season to another. In early 2006, Amaranth theorized that mild weather and a growing glut of natural gas would cause prices to decline in the fall of the year, only to be reversed by increased demand for gas in the winter months. To express this fundamental view, the fund amassed two major positions in the spring of 2006. The first trade involved a short position of nearly 30,000 June natural gas futures contracts,[10] a nearly $3 billion bet (assuming gas prices of $10 per million BTU) that gas prices would decline in the next few months. This trade was remarkable for both its size—Amaranth routinely owned roughly one-third of all positions on the exchange—and the short window it allowed for the position to perform.

The second involved a "January/November calendar spread" that consisted of selling contracts for the delivery of natural gas in November 2006 and buying contracts for natural gas delivery in January 2007. This represented a bet that prices in January would increase relative to November, causing the spread to widen.

As shown in Figure 5-2, when Amaranth placed these trades, significant seasonal price differences were already evident in the contracts: the price for gas delivery in January was nearly $1 higher than the contracts for November delivery. Through its trades, Amaranth was effectively betting that these spreads would not only stay wide but further increase.

Consistent with the fund's growing swagger, Amaranth and Hunter pursued these calendar spread strategies in extreme proportions. On most days in early 2006, Amaranth also held more than 50% of the open interest (total outstanding contracts) in the January 2007 and November 2006 contracts. By late April, the combination of Amaranth's ~$3 billion short June position; a 30,000/34,000 contract November/January spread totaling more than $6 billion in exposure; and a host of other long and short positions in the fund created a gross exposure to natural gas that totaled over $10 billion. To put this in perspective, this represented contracts to buy and sell well over 1 trillion cubic feet of natural gas, or approximately 25% of the natural gas consumed by all U.S. households in 2006.[11] To achieve these epic levels of risk, Amaranth made several trips to the leverage buffet, apparently employing somewhere between five and eight times the investor equity capital employed.[12]

The Roach Motel Problem

As 2006 unfolded, the enormous size of these bets quickly over-shadowed other strategies the fund was pursuing; energy now was the fund's dominant strategy, representing over 50% of its capital by the middle of the year.[13] With this transformation, in the span of several months, Amaranth effectively had placed much of its fate in the hands of a 32-year-old trader.

By the end of April, the gamble appeared to be a paying off. In that month alone, the spread between the November 2006 and January 2007 contracts had widened from $1.59 to $2.22. The short June contract also did well, as the price of the contract fell from $7.42 to $6.55. All told, Amaranth's energy portfolio gained more than $1 billion during the month, making it the dominant contributor to the fund's 14% return for April and its cumulative 30% gain year to date in 2006.[14] See Table 5-2.

In its monthly letter for April, Amaranth described the drivers behind its success:

> Our energy and commodities portfolios generated outsized returns due to unusual volatility across the crude oil, natural gas and metals businesses. Primary drivers of the returns included (1) natural gas spread trades, which benefited from the significant increase in crude oil prices and the glut of summer 2006 natural gas relative to

Table 5-2 Amaranth Returns, January to April 2006

Month	Monthly Return	Year-to-Date Return
January	6.45%	6.45%
February	4.30%	11.03%
March	2.91%	14.26%
April	14.42%	30.73%

storage capacity and prospective summer demand, and (2) a profound increase in base metals prices (copper in particular) with an associate volatility spike. As volatility increased during the month, we took the opportunity to reduce exposure in our natural gas and metals portfolios and realized profits.

Perhaps the most interesting aspect of this letter is Amaranth's attributing its outsized returns primarily to "unusual volatility." This "volatility" was most likely heavily influenced by the massive buying and selling efforts of the fund itself, which had established roughly $5 billion of long and short positions for the November/January spread, representing approximately 60% of all outstanding contracts. In other words, the more January contracts Amaranth bought, the higher the price went, and the more November contracts they sold, the further its price fell, together increasing the calendar spread in which Amaranth was long. With the enormous size of its trades and accompanying market share dominance, Amaranth was arguably helping to create its own profits.

A United States Senate investigation on excessive speculation in the natural gas market seemed to support this supposition when it found that the correlation between the size of Amaranth's spread positions and the price of the spread from January to the end of April was 0.93:

> Because Amaranth was overwhelmingly the predominant buyer of January contracts and the predominant seller of November contracts during this period, meaning that it was the predominant buyer of the January/November spread, its actions must be considered to be the predominant cause of the increase in the January/November price spread.

Given Amaranth's enormous buying power, generating unrealized gains in the process of establishing its own trades would have been the easy part. However, much like a roach motel, exiting these positions and realizing the gains would prove a far more difficult task. In mid-May, Amaranth tried to realize some of its gains by selling positions. However, the process of establishing such large positions apparently so exaggerated prices that the fund found few players willing to take them out of their trades. Making matters worse, other large sellers emerged to take advantage of the high prices that existed in many of their contracts. By late May, as a consequence of these forces, the market started to move against Amaranth. The spread between the January and November contracts fell nearly 20%, from $2.15 to $1.73, contributing to a loss of more than $1.1 billion for the firm.[15] Despite Amaranth's apparent desire to reduce its position size and lock in remaining profits, the sheer size of its investments prohibited an easy exit from the roach motel. In its monthly letter to investors for May 2006, the fund described the liquidity problem it faced:

> Historically, the market has provided sufficient liquidity and opportunity for us to tailor the portfolio as desired despite rapidly changing market dynamics. This "expansion/contraction" approach has enabled us to generate more profits than if we had required the team to unwind trades aggressively whenever markets moved in our favor. In this case, as we endeavored to monetize gains (and reduce risk) within the portfolio, liquidity in the portfolio seized up due to high volumes of producer hedging that oversaturated market demand for forward natural gas. While this was a humbling experience that has led us to recalibrate how we assess risk in this business, we believe certain spread relationships remain disconnected from their fundamental value drivers.

Bad news travels fast in the hedge fund industry and the commodities market, and it's especially hard to keep a billion-dollar loss quiet. Once word got out, it wouldn't have been difficult for the market to figure out who had lost the money and what the approximate size of their positions were. This only served to shrink the roach motel exit a few sizes smaller.

According to subsequent conversations between Amaranth employees and regulators, there were discussions within the firm about whether or not Amaranth should try to unwind positions at a substantial discount to market prices and take another loss, estimated at an additional $1 billion. Unfortunately for Amaranth, they didn't. "We thought about pulling the trigger and taking the loss," an Amaranth trader said. "We had many discussions about it. We figured we could get out for maybe a billion dollars. But we decided to ride it out and see if the market would come around."[16]

The Widow Maker

In fact, instead of reducing risk, they did just the opposite; they increased their positions, substantially. By the end of July, Amaranth's long positions in the January 2007 contract had grown to 80,000 contracts. The short fall leg of this fall/winter spread bet had been rolled to October and maintained at approximately 40,000 contracts. The fund's other short bet on natural gas had been rolled to September and increased to nearly 60,000 contracts. Amaranth also initiated a new trade, this time a position that bet on the spread between two consecutive months, March and April 2007. Normally the spread between any two consecutive months is quite narrow and not particularly volatile. These two months, however, represented the end of winter (March) and the first month of summer (April) in the gas market. Given the uncertainty surrounding the amount of gas remaining in storage and the outlook for summer heat, the spread between these two months is generally considered to be among the most volatile. In fact, the risk associated with this spread is so high that it is ominously referred to as the "widow makers bet."[17]

Amaranth put on the widow maker, in size: 59,000 contracts long for March and 80,000 short contracts for April.[18] Given the massive size of these bets and the risk involved, Amaranth seemed to be putting its chips "all in." Unfortunately for the fund's investors, the cards would not deliver a reversal of fortune.

The End Game

The trouble began at the expiration of the September contract, in which Amaranth was short. On the day of expiration, August 29, 2006, the price rose approximately $0.60 in the last hour of trading, which, along with other positions, resulted in a loss of nearly $600 million for the day. Even for a fund of Amaranth's size, this was a particularly bad day at the office. The very next week, the two critical long spreads upon which Amaranth had bet the ranch—the March/April and January/October spreads—started to narrow as well.

The spread between the March and April 2007 contracts, for example, went from roughly $2.50 at the end of August to just above $0.50 three weeks later. The January/October spread followed a similar path, falling from $4.68 on September 1 to $3.52 two weeks later. The sharp decline of these spreads, in many ways, marked the beginning of the end for Amaranth.[19]

As the losses mounted over the course of September, the fund's margin requirements had eclipsed $3 billion.[20] The magnitude of these losses and the additional capital required to maintain the positions meant that Amaranth could no longer support its positions as it had done in the past. Essentially, the fund had run out of poker chips. With their pockets empty, they were now at the mercy of the market.

Faced with billions in margin calls and a rapidly deteriorating situation in the fund's gas positions, Amaranth began to seek counterparties to bid for its positions. The size and market dominance of Amaranth's positions—in some contracts, Amaranth's positions were larger than the entire rest of the market, combined—meant that the process wasn't going to be pretty. The first bid they received was from John Arnold, CEO of another hedge fund, Centaurus. His bid was roughly 50% of the current value of certain contracts.[21] He offered the bid with the following assessment of Amaranth's situation:

> I was not in the office on Friday but I understand you were selling h/j [March/April]. The market is now [so] loaded up on recent, bad purchases that they will probably try to be spitting out on Monday if there is a lower opening, given the spread has been in free fall. In my opinion, fundamentally, that spread is still a long way from fundamental value.

He went on to say,

> Over the past couple of years the market has put a big risk premium into that spread yet it has paid out on expiry once in ten years. We'll be at all time high storage levels with mediocre s/p [supply/demand] and an el nino. Even though your spread has collapsed over the

past two weeks, the only reason it's still $1 is because of your position. Historically, that spread would be well below $1 at this point given the scenario.[22]

After days of intense negotiations with banks, broker dealers, and hedge funds, Amaranth sold its energy portfolio to its clearing broker, J.P. Morgan, and Citadel Investment Group. Investor losses eventually totaled more than $6 billion, or approximately 65% of the fund's NAV.

The Aftermath

Maounis offered the following explanation during an investor conference in late September:

> Although the size of our natural gas exposures was large, we believed, based on input from both our trading desk and the stress-testing performed by our energy risk team that the amount of risk capital ascribed to the natural gas portfolio was sufficient.
>
> In September 2006, a series of unusual and unpredictable market events caused the Funds' natural gas positions (including spreads) to incur dramatic losses while the markets provided no economically viable means of exiting those positions. Despite all of our efforts, we were unable to close out the exposures in the public markets. Market conditions deteriorated rapidly during the week of September 11. Material losses began early in the week, and we accelerated our efforts to reduce our exposures. On Thursday, September 14, the Funds experienced roughly $560 million in trading losses on their natural gas positions. We continued to attempt to reduce our natural gas exposures, while also selling other positions to raise cash in order

to meet margin calls. As news of our losses began to sweep through the markets, our already limited access to market liquidity quickly dissipated.

The illiquidity of the public market made it clear that we could not rely on these markets to trade out of the natural gas positions quickly enough to protect the Funds. Recognizing this, we immediately began actively contacting financial institutions which we thought had the resources and interest to take on Amaranth's natural gas exposures—*and* could act within the limited time frame available to us . . .

Our September losses were caused by a combination of highly unusual market behavior—not simply adverse price movements— that not only eroded the energy book's capital but also virtually eliminated the firm's liquidity. We had not expected that we would be faced with a market that would move so aggressively against our positions without the market offering any ability to liquidate positions economically.

We viewed the probability of market movements such as those that took place in September as highly remote, and our energy-risk models correspondingly discount the Funds' exposures to the losses associated with such scenarios. In addition, the trading desk expressed confidence that we would be able to achieve our position reduction goals economically and expeditiously. But sometimes, even the highly improbable happens. That is what happened in September.

Was the downfall of Amaranth a consequence of the hedge fund Peter Principle? During an investor conference call, Maounis appeared to try to address the question:

It goes without saying that these losses were contrary to your expectations as well as our own. It was not, however, for lack of applying resources or personnel to energy risk analysis that our funds experienced this severe drawdown. For as long as we have had a significant energy business, we have assigned full-time, well-credentialed and experienced risk professionals to model and monitor our energy portfolio's risks.

How could our Multi-Strategy Fund have acquired such a large allocation to energy? Amaranth has, since inception, from time to time opportunistically made large allocations to certain strategies — merger arbitrage and convertibles, for example. It is fully consistent with the multi-strategy approach we have applied since inception to make large allocations from time to time. Nor was the Fund's energy exposures a new development. Throughout 2005 and continuing into 2006, the Funds were well-known to have growing energy market exposures. For example, as reported in the monthly "snapshot" distributed to investors for February 28, approximately 39% of the Fund's capital was allocated to the energy and commodities portfolio.

Maounis's comments acknowledge a major shift away from the fund's previous core strategies and into energy. Were these new energy investments well understood and effectively monitored by the risk team and senior management? You'll have to be the judge.

In November 2007, Amaranth filed a lawsuit against J.P. Morgan, seeking more than a billion dollars in damages arising from the bank's role in losses suffered by the fund. In a letter to investors, Maounis defended his fund and placed a substantial portion of the blame for its troubles on J.P. Morgan:

While the Fund's losses have frequently been described in the financial press as "trading" losses, the fact of the matter is that over $2.5 billion of those losses resulted directly from a cash concession payment required by J.P. Morgan in connection with taking over the Fund's energy derivatives portfolio. The attached Complaint recounts how J.P. Morgan used its position as the Fund's clearing broker to prevent the Fund from executing more favorable transactions, to extract that massive concession payment and inflict other damages on the Fund. It is our view that absent J.P. Morgan's actions, the Fund's losses, though significant, would have been survivable and far less dramatic.

In response to Amaranth's suit, J.P. Morgan said in a statement: "Amaranth's lawsuit is an effort to rewrite history, and to blame J.P. Morgan for losses that were the result of Amaranth's disastrous trading. J.P. Morgan's conduct was entirely appropriate."[23]

Ultimately, the courts will determine just what J.P. Morgan's role was. However the blame is ultimately shared, perhaps the most remarkable part of this story is that with roughly $9 billion under management, the senior executives of Amaranth allowed a golden goose, laying more than $200 million a year in compensation eggs, to be slaughtered.

Fortunately, not all funds that grow rapidly experience the pain of Amaranth. Many, such as Och-Ziff, Highbridge, and many others, have managed to diversify into other strategies and continue to successfully manage the expanded risk profile of the larger fund. For most of these funds, success has undoubtedly been rooted, at least in part, in a very disciplined approach to the management of key risk factors including leverage, maximum position limits, strategy concentration, asset type concentration, geographic concentration, and position level liquidity.

Perhaps the lesson for investors is this: If you are invested in a fund that is doubling its assets every year or two and, at the same time, diversifying into new strategies with new teams of portfolio managers, then you should assume that the risk profile of the fund is rising just as fast as the assets. While you are listening to the manager assure you that all of the fund's new strategies are "related," and the massively larger and more diverse fund will in no way dilute his ability to deliver attractive returns, you may just want to pause and consider whether this is still the best opportunity around.

six

CAPITAL INSTABILITY AND ILLIQUIDITY

A TOXIC COMBINATION

It took just ten years for hedge funds to evolve from a cottage industry, with thousands of independent managers at small firms, into a densely concentrated group of multibillion-dollar, well-established institutions. In 2008, just 390 hedge funds held roughly $2.5 trillion of industry assets—80% of the total[1]—with each managing an average of $5 billion. In a decent year, most of them can easily clear $150 million in operating income.

Most corporations generating this kind of money have established stable, multilevel capital structures. The majority have some type of permanent equity capital, which supports a layer of multiyear term bank debt or other form of longer-dated debt.

In the hedge fund world, the capital structures have not, for the most part, kept pace with the huge growth of AUM. In fact, with the exception of a handful of hedge fund IPOs and medium-term note offerings, debt financing remains similar to what you can get in a personal Fidelity account: short-term, brokerage-style margin financing. The equity capital underlying these businesses is equally fleeting, with lockups averaging only three months.

This would be fine if all hedge funds focused on long-short equity, dealing in actively traded shares, but this isn't the case. Based on information from Hedge Fund Research, Inc., in 2008, roughly 65% of hedge funds were pursuing strategies other than long-short equity. Within these funds, there are many strategies targeting long-dated investments in corporate bonds, bank debt, convertible securities, CLOs, CDOs, asset-backed securities, distressed debt, and other securities.

Chapter 2 examined the litany of risks that accompany the financing of these longer-term assets with short-term, prime brokerage financing: inopportune liquidations, forced asset sales, and fire sales, to name a few. With its daily margin requirements, NAV triggers, and possibility of unilateral termination, prime brokerage financing can often spell disaster for managers holding longer-term, less-liquid assets.

Interestingly, in the three cases of catastrophic collapse discussed here—Sowood, Bear, and Amaranth—the investment losses and margin call/covenant breaches occurred so quickly that few investors in the funds had time to withdraw any equity capital. Nearly everyone had to share the pain. In many other situations, however, the loss of debt and equity capital occurs over a much longer period of time. In these cases, the stability of a fund's equity capital is key to both its ongoing investment performance and, ultimately, its survival.

As further detailed in Chapter 2, the debt and equity capital of a fund are inextricably connected through the NAV debt covenant.

This trigger allows the debt of a hedge fund to be terminated if the fund's NAV—calculated using both investment performance and investor capital additions and withdrawals—falls by a set percentage, usually between 10% and 30%. Given the role that equity capital plays in this calculation, it is important to understand both the factors that lead to equity capital instability and the mechanisms hedge funds use to try to control it.

Hedge Fund Equity Capital

According to HedgeFund.net, for the six months ending in December 2008, the hedge fund industry lost approximately $1 trillion in equity capital, over a third of the total amount invested. Of this amount, roughly $500 to $600 billion probably can be chalked up to investment losses; the rest came from investor redemptions. Despite the staggering size of these capital losses, they occurred while 30% to 40% of all hedge funds were limiting investor withdrawals through a variety of means, including gate mechanisms, suspensions, and restructurings. If all investors who were seeking liquidity at that time could have gotten it, some estimate that another $500 billion more would have disappeared, bringing the total investor withdrawals to somewhere around $1 trillion.

If this estimate is correct, it suggests that roughly one-third of all of the capital in the hedge fund industry was seeking an exit at the end of 2008.

Where did all of these redemption requests come from? Was one investor group more responsible than others? The answer to these questions can be found in a better understanding of the source and stability of capital held by each category of hedge fund investor.

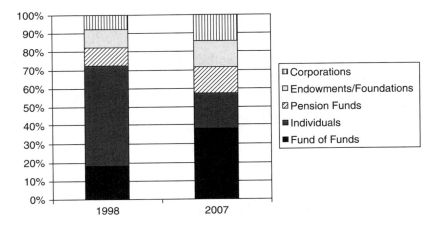

Figure 6-1 Hedge fund sources of capital
Source: AIMA, other industry estimates for 2007

Hedge fund investors generally fall into one of five categories: funds of hedge funds, high net worth individuals, pension funds, corporations, and endowments and foundations. As Figure 6-1 highlights, fund of funds (FOFs) have grown to represent the largest source of capital for the industry, about 40% of the $2.9 trillion total. Much of this growth has been fueled by demand from pensions and other institutional investors. High net worth investors, at 20%, make up the second largest group. The rest of the sources represent roughly 15% each.

Funds of Hedge Funds

The credit crisis ushered in a harsh new reality for this group, once the largest and fastest growing. It appears to have lost more capital than any other investor category, its fees are increasingly under pressure, and the involvement of FOFs in several large frauds has cast an unflattering light on many within the group.

In general, these funds act as a sort of intermediary, managing a portfolio of hedge fund investments for a variety of investors who don't have the resources, sophistication, capital, or time to do so on their own. Investors in an FOF typically have paid a fee of 1% on AUM (the management fee) and 10% of any positive performance. This fee buys the investor a variety of key investment services: hedge fund manager selection, monitoring, risk management, strategy weighting, and capital aggregation for those who don't have enough capital to meet the minimum investment thresholds required to create a diversified portfolio of direct hedge fund investments.

Early on, much of the capital invested in FOFs came from individuals. More recently, however, pensions and other institutional investors, given their massive allocation increases to alternative investments, have represented a substantially larger share.

Prior to the credit crisis, the allure of FOFs was hard for hedge fund managers to resist. FOFs tended to invest quickly—usually in less than six months from introduction to investment—and they did not typically require a long track record before investing. Their allocations tended to be substantial. For a $10 to $20 billion FOF, investments of less than $100 to $200 million were both too small to "move the needle" of their investment performance and administratively too costly to monitor. As a result, FOFs alone could take a hedge fund with reasonably attractive performance from a few hundred million under management to a few billion in the span of a year or less. In short, FOFs provided quick, certain access to billions in AUM and a chance to drink from the industry's fire hose of fees.

But many saw the downside of FOF capital in the fall of 2008. It was hot money, inherently short-term capital that fled at the first sign of trouble. There were several reasons for this. First, much of the capital managed by an FOF is itself fleeting. FOFs typically provide their investors with the option to withdraw capital on a quarterly or even monthly basis. With its own capital at risk month to month, an FOF naturally is more focused on a hedge fund's recent absolute and relative investment performance than would be a pension, endowment, or other investor whose investment horizon is measured in years or even decades.

Adding to this problem, some FOFs face an inherent redemption/liquidity timing mismatch in their portfolios. This occurs when an FOF provides its investors with monthly or quarterly redemption rights but invests in hedge funds that provide liquidity on a quarterly or yearly basis. The FOFs knowingly accept this risk, betting that any investor redemption requests will be light enough that they will always be able to generate enough cash from their hedge fund investments to cover them. Their ability to do so, however, depends on being able to access capital in the portion of their hedge fund portfolio that allows near term liquidity. Thus, if an FOF gets "extended" by the imposition of gates or other mechanisms that slow the return of investor capital in its hedge fund investments, the liquidity mismatch problem can be exacerbated. In the extreme, it can prevent the FOF from meeting redemption requests from its underlying investors, causing a suspension or other restriction on redemptions. As a result, in times of stress, some FOFs will quickly redeem hedge funds in an attempt to build cash "cushions" to better manage any liquidity mismatch that may exist.

The final factor in the FOF equation is, once again, our old friend leverage. Many managers just don't feel they can compete without it. For an FOF with 1.5, 2, or 3 times leverage that's invested in hedge funds with 2, 3, or 4 times leverage, any bump in the road results in pain squared. And just as with a hedge fund, when poor performance rears its ugly head, a short lockup will only encourage greater redemptions.

The fall of 2008 represented a near perfect storm for many FOFs. Leverage and poor performance contributed to redemption requests totaling 30% to 40% of total FOF capital. At the same time, the underlying hedge fund investments of FOFs, also facing massive redemptions, began suspending or restricting investors' rights to redeem. By year end, at least 30% to 40% of all hedge funds had restricted investor redemptions in some way, severely limiting FOF access to cash. As a result, a number of FOFs, including Permal Investment Management, Mellon Global Alternative Investments, and Lafayette Investment Management, were unable to meet their own redemption requests and opted to limit cash outflows through a variety of mechanisms. Overall, the FOF group of investors probably accounted for proportionally more of the 2008 capital outflows from the hedge fund industry than any other. In the future, given the short lockups FOFs provide to their investors and the accompanying liquidity mismatch they sometimes create, this investor group seems destined to remain renters of hedge funds rather than long-term owners.

High Net Worth Investors

High net worth investors, like FOFs, also tend to fall into the hot money category of hedge fund investors. Unlike FOFs, however, they are, by definition, investing their own capital. With the exception of large, well-organized family offices, these investors lack both the capital required to become major investors in a hedge fund and the resources to diligently monitor a portfolio of complex investments. Consequently, many invest based on manager perception, historical returns, and personal connections.

It's a fine approach on calm seas, but imagine a high net worth investor in late 2008, pondering his or her portfolio of hedge fund investments: returns are down more than 20% for the year, several funds have blown up from excessive leverage and bad investments, banks are pulling back capital, industry redemptions are reportedly at record levels, and Bernard Madoff has just been caught at the largest fraud ever committed.

For many, the decision was easy—redeem ASAP. Like FOFs, high net worth investors were also large redeemers of hedge fund capital in 2008.

Pension Funds and Endowments

Fortunately for the hedge fund industry, pension funds, endowments, and other institutional investors are different. Over the past 5 to 10 years, state pension funds and university endowments have increasingly become direct investors in hedge funds. Unlike FOFs, these institutional investors commit their own capital with a view toward meeting longer-term pension benefit payouts or endowment obligations. As a result, they tend to view the performance of their hedge fund investments over a similarly long time horizon. This perspective is mainly a function of the liabilities under a fund's umbrella. If a manager knows that his liabilities have a duration of 5 or 10 years, he's likely to view the performance of his assets over the same period. Also, the boards of these funds often seek to compensate their managers with a multiyear performance assessment system rather than an annual model. With this investment approach, pension, endowment, and other institutional investors have provided a more stable source of capital for hedge funds.

The trade-off, however, is a much more extensive diligence process. Few pension or endowment funds will invest in a hedge fund start-up, and few will commit without at least a two- or three-year track record. They will also seek additional transparency, fee reductions, and other perks in exchange for the stability they offer. These demands may seem onerous, but this is the price for stability, the holy grail of hedge fund equity capital.

A Run on the Bank

All smart hedge funds seek a diversified and reliable pool of equity capital, but not all of them attain this key objective. Without it, the risk of triggering a fund's NAV debt covenant in times of stress is much higher, raising the possibility of lost debt financing and forced asset sales. Even if the NAV trigger isn't tripped, uncontrolled large equity redemptions can lead to uneconomic asset sales and an increased concentration of less liquid investments in the portfolio; both of which leave nonredeeming investors at a disadvantage.

To address these risks, hedge funds have come up with a load of mechanisms to control the rate at which equity capital can leave the fund. That the hedge fund industry would design clever devices to prevent the escape of the golden goose is no surprise. What did surprise many investors, however, was the unintended "run on the bank" that many of these devices incited when they were rolled out on a broad scale in late 2008.

The first and most basic mechanism is the lockup. Most hedge funds ask investors for a one-year initial lockup, but, depending on the type of assets managed and the strength of the manager, they might ask for two years or more. Once this time has expired, investors typically have the right to request redemption of their shares at the end of any calendar quarter going forward. To give the manager time to generate the cash, most funds require a notice period of approximately 30 to 60 days.

For many new funds experiencing tremendous capital growth, this structure provides built-in stability for all or a portion of the fund's capital for the length of the lockup period. However, as a fund matures and these initial lockups roll off, the majority of its equity capital becomes "at risk" every quarter.

During the credit crisis, this 60-day notice period was an edgy time for many funds. They were forced to begin selling assets to raise cash, despite being unsure how many assets they actually needed to sell. The tension derived from a "rescission option" embedded in the lockup notice period, which allowed investors to rescind their redemption request at any time during the notice period. Despite the fact that most hedge fund documents say that redemption requests are irrevocable, the desire to retain investor capital meant that most rescission requests were granted. As a result, even though a 60-day notice was required, hedge funds didn't know the actual amount of cash they would have to pay until much later in the process.

This wasn't their only problem. In a classic case of unintended consequences, many of the other mechanisms they created to slow the exodus of capital contained a host of incentives that actually encouraged investors to redeem.

Rushing the Gate

On the surface, the hedge fund gate has a simple purpose: limit the number of investor withdrawals in any given period to keep the downsizing of portfolio assets manageable and limit the impact of asset sales on investment performance. In order to accomplish this, gates are typically structured to limit withdrawals at 15% of AUM, but the percentage can vary between 5% and 25%.

A gate can also help to manage the NAV trigger problem by allowing the fund to limit the redemptions to a level below the monthly threshold for termination by financing counterparties. Hedge funds deliberately set the gate's threshold at or below their monthly NAV trigger. As an example, assume a fund sets both its gate threshold and monthly NAV trigger at 15% of NAV. If the fund received and paid cash for redemption notices totaling 20% of its NAV, the fund would be in default of all of its financing agreements. However, before this would happen, the fund would simply invoke its gate, thereby limiting redemptions to 15% and forestalling the default. Alas, this theoretical scenario assumes performance is stable when redemptions are high—a relatively rare event in the real world, where poor performance and investor redemptions tend to go hand in hand (funny how that works). For most funds, an NAV trigger event typically includes both investor redemptions and declines in assets due to poor performance. In these cases, the gate won't always prevent an NAV covenant breach.

Importantly, the gate is also designed to help the hedge fund manager manage the composition of the portfolio. One of the key fiduciary responsibilities of a hedge fund manager facing redemptions is to treat both exiting and remaining investors fairly. The most challenging aspect of maintaining this fairness arises when a hedge fund manager seeks to raise cash for redemptions by selling securities. The most liquid positions, such as stocks and convertible securities, typically have the lowest haircuts (most leverage) in the portfolio, and thus when sold generate the least cash (because little was required to be posted originally). As a result, if the manager isn't careful, she will end up selling proportionally more of the liquid assets, leaving the remaining investors with a less liquid and perhaps less desirable portfolio. In the same way, liquidation can also leave remaining investors with a less than optimal overall allocation to the fund's core strategies.

The gate feature attempts to mitigate these portfolio composition problems by limiting the amount of redemptions in any quarterly period. However, the extent to which a gate can address this condition depends on the proportion of illiquid assets in the portfolio. When illiquid assets make up a substantial portion of the portfolio—common enough in 2008—some funds have a separate fund called a "side pocket," which can be used to hold illiquid investments on behalf of all investors and better address the proportionate exposure issue. More on this later.

Getting Stacked

Paradoxically, the gate mechanism at its core can contain one of the strongest incentives for investors to redeem, even if they do not have an immediate need for cash. Many hedge fund gates are designed with a "stacking" feature. It requires the fund to aggregate all redemption requests for a quarterly period and then satisfy a portion of those requests based on the gate payout percentage.

Any requests that have not been satisfied (the amount that is higher than the gate threshold) are then rolled over to the next redemption date and are redeemed either fully or partially *before* any subsequent redemption requests for the next period are considered.

So if an investor suspects a significant amount of redemption requests may be submitted to a fund, and if that fund has a stacking gate, the investor has major incentive to submit a redemption request to avoid being stacked and thereby shut out of any cash withdrawals until all earlier requests have been satisfied.

In the fall of 2008, redemption requests were so common that some investors who didn't put in a request for the June or September quarter were so low in the stack that they wouldn't get a penny of their capital back for up to a year or more. For FOFs and other investors facing substantial capital redemptions of their own, this stacking risk all but required them to place significant redemption requests with most of their hedge fund managers.

Nonstacking gates attempt to avoid this problem by funneling all new requests in any given quarter and unsatisfied requests from earlier quarters into a single pool, against which the gate payout formula is applied. In this case, all investors who are seeking to redeem participate each quarter on a pro rata basis, removing the incentive to redeem just to maintain a spot in the queue. Nonstacking gates, however, clearly disadvantage smarter investors who have the foresight to see problems at a fund before others.

Whether a gate is structured as stacking or nonstacking, the outcome for investors seeking return of capital is the same: limited current access to cash and an uncertain timetable for the return of their remaining investment.

Smart investors understand this, and they get nervous when they see these factors coming into play simultaneously. In extreme cases, it can begin a downward spiral that is hard to reverse.

Once a gate is actually utilized, investors must contend with a host of new worries:

1. *Future redemption requests.* As we've discussed, gate mechanisms leave investors with uncertain future access to capital in both timing and amount. For many, this uncertainty forces them to put in additional redemption requests to "get in line" for whatever future payouts will be made by the hedge fund. As a consequence, utilization of a gate often begets significant additional future redemption requests.

2. *The impact of asset sales on performance.* In order to generate cash to pay redemptions, most funds must sell assets. Once this process begins, investors face the possibility that the liquidation will negatively impact the performance of existing positions.

3. *Underinvestment.* Once a gate has been imposed, many managers seek to retain larger amounts of cash in the fund to defend against potential future redemption requests, leading to a systematic underinvestment in attractive market opportunities.

4. *Loss of debt financing.* The loss of equity capital, potential additional redemption requests, and poor performance often associated with a gate increases the risk of future NAV debt covenant breaches.

5. The potential for defection of key investment professionals as assets decline.

6. The risk that a manager may "swing for the fences" during this period, taking on high-risk investments in an effort to save the fund.

With all of these issues, it is not surprising that many investors consider the imposition of a gate a highly negative event. Many believe that the potential for additional redemption requests, lost financing, assets sales, poor investment performance, and other negative events increase the probability of a self-fulfilling downward spiral for the fund.

Suspension of Redemptions

The situation can get even uglier for investors when the rush to redeem strikes a fund carrying a large proportion of illiquid assets. A gate mechanism offers little help when a fund has a limited ability to generate cash and a substantial risk of unfairly saddling remaining investors with illiquid assets. For these situations, funds can be forced to turn to another far more draconian option: suspension of redemptions altogether.

In the documents of most funds, a provision exists that typically says the fund "may suspend redemption rights in whole or in part, when there exists a state of affairs where disposal of the fund's assets would not be reasonably practicable or would be seriously prejudicial to the nonredeeming shareholders." In other words, if things get bad enough, the fund will suspend redemptions entirely, locking up all investor capital *indefinitely*.

In hedge fund investing, the gate is considered a serious but fairly conventional form of weaponry. Suspension, however, is the equivalent of going nuclear. It gives the manager and the board of directors the discretion to hold investor capital and continue to receive management fees (also indefinitely) without any objective tests to confirm the necessity of the measure. The longer the suspension, the more likely that most if not all capital will leave when it is lifted.

In the fall of 2008, with hedge fund performance down for the year by 25%, banks pulling leverage, widespread market illiquidity, and steep losses in other asset classes, the average hedge fund received redemption requests for 30% to 40% of its assets. Given the size of these requests and the illiquidity that existed in many markets, perhaps it is understandable that at least 30% to 40% of all hedge funds either brought down a gate or suspended redemptions altogether.

As Table 6-1 highlights, the funds that resorted to these tactics included some of the largest and most prominent in the industry: D.E. Shaw, Fortress Investment Group, Citadel Investment Group, and Tudor, among others.

Table 6-1 Major Hedge Fund Gates or Suspensions, 2008–2009

Blue Mountain Capital	Highbridge Capital Management
Centaurus Capital	Lydian Asset Management
Cerberus Capital Management	Plainfield Asset
Citadel Investment Group	Polygon Investment Partners
D.E. Shaw Group	RAB Capital
Deephaven Capital Management	Satellite Asset Management
Farallon Capital Management	Steele Partners
Fortress Investment Group	Tudor BVI Fund
GLG Partners	Whitebox Advisors

Note: Managers at firms on the list utilized a gate or suspension feature in at least one fund.

What this data does not convey, however, is that gate and suspension provisions were far more common among funds with less liquid strategies, such as relative value credit funds, distressed debt funds, multi-strategy managers, convertible arbitrage funds, and activist strategies.

Funds focused on more liquid strategies, like many long-short equity funds, liquid macro strategies, and commodity investments, rarely gated or suspended redemptions. That doesn't mean these funds didn't field any redemption requests. In most cases, they did, even if they made money in 2008. With so many hedge funds resorting to gate or suspension tactics, any fund that pursued a liquid investment strategy and had access to cash became an ATM for cash starved investors. These funds were in a much better position to return capital to investors; after they received notice of redemptions, they simply entered the market, sold assets, and paid out the cash.

For the rest, illiquid assets, leverage, and unstable equity created a problem that would not go away easily. Gates and suspension mechanisms provided temporary relief, but given their tendency to incite significantly more redemptions in the following quarters, a longer-term solution was needed.

Hedge Fund 2.0: Restructuring

As 2008 drew to a close, it became clear that market liquidity for many seized-up assets wasn't likely to improve quickly. At the same time, investors, many with their own pressing cash needs, wanted their capital back and were becoming increasingly impatient about it. As these pressures increased, many funds realized that their ability to survive the crisis would diminish significantly without a long-term plan.

For many, the answer was to completely restructure their funds. In the chaos of 2008, there were dozens of variations on the restructuring model as managers searched for something that might work. Despite the spaghetti-on-the-wall nature of these strategies, a couple of common elements emerged. First was the creation or use of a separate side pocket fund for truly illiquid, toxic assets for which no reasonably priced market existed. Second, funds tended to provide investors with two options: (1) waive your redemptions rights and go into a liquidating share class that would, depending on market conditions, attempt to return investor capital over the course of approximately six months to one year, or (2) transfer to an ongoing investment fund and agree to a new, one year (or longer) lockup with lower fees or other enticements.

For many stressed funds, this model made the best of a bad situation. The side pocket addressed the issue of illiquid assets by proportionally allocating them between redeeming and ongoing investors. Through the liquidating fund, the plan generated cash for investors that wanted it, and for remaining investors, it allowed the fund to maintain a stable investment platform going forward.

But while this strategy created a new box for the illiquid assets, they didn't disappear. Investors still owned them, and by all accounts they will continue to for some time. Most side pockets allowed hedge fund managers to place as much as 25% of the fund's total AUM into a special account that is *nonredeemable* by investors. Because this vehicle is essentially a separate fund designed for long-term liquidation of illiquid assets, investors can't get out except through manager liquidation of assets.

The Structured Securities Liquidity Mirage

As painful as it is for an investor to be stuck in a side pocket indefinitely, there are good reasons why past investment mistakes should reside inside them. Consider, for example, the story of corporate bank loan CLO debt, once a popular hedge fund investment that now lines many a side pocket.

CLOs were vehicles established by credit managers or hedge funds to purchase large pools of corporate bank loans. These loan pools served as collateral for a variety of debt and equity securities that were sold to investors, each offering different tranches of risk and return on the performance of the underlying loan pool.

In early 2006, the majority of these tranched CLO securities were highly liquid. Banks and broker-dealers eagerly made active markets for a broad spectrum of hedge funds, institutional credit managers, and other investors. By late 2008, however, "structured" securities had become the bane of Wall Street. Subprime mortgage CDO securities already had destroyed a number of banks and hedge funds, and anything even loosely related to them was considered toxic. Banks would not finance CLO debt, investors didn't want to own it, brokers refused to make a market in the securities, and liquidity was virtually nonexistent. For many securities, it was impossible even to get a reasonable price quote in the market.

The situation with the BBB-rated CLO tranches highlighted the problem. With the overall bank loan market trading at around 60% of par in early 2009, buyers of BBB-rated, investment-grade tranches were willing to pay 5% to 10% of par, whereas sellers were offering to sell at 25% to 30% of par. As a result, nothing was traded; price was effectively in the eye of the beholder.

Table 6-2 Major Hedge Fund Side Pockets, 2008–2009

Atticus Capital
Diamondback Capital
GLG Partners
Golden Tree Asset Management
Highbridge Capital Management
JANA Partners
SAC Capital
Sandell Asset Management
Sandelman Partners
Scoggin Capital

Note: Managers at firms on the list utilized a side pocket in at least one fund.

In some cases, a side pocket forced to sell a large amount of BBB CLO debt in this environment may have received less than 5% of par, a tough price at the time for even the most pessimistic seller.

As painful as side pockets are for investors, they are probably the best place for deeply illiquid assets. Still, for many investors who invested in hedge funds with the expectation of quarterly liquidity, these vehicles have become an unwelcome headache on 15% to 25% of their capital.

Carl Icahn Sues His Hedge Fund

Given the large number of hedge fund restructurings that occurred in 2008, there were bound to be a number of exceptions to the basic framework outlined earlier. In general, the plans that went "off the reservation" tended to involve a more complex attempt to reach for longer-term or even permanent capital, better fees, and other advantages for the manager. In the tense climate of 2008, however, investors were in no mood for science experiments. Any perceived delay in the return of capital or other inequality was likely to incur the wrath of an already bloodied and highly agitated investor community.

Among the outliers, few concocted plans were more polarizing than Steel Partners.

Steel Partners is a roughly $2.5 billion activist hedge fund run by Warren Lichtenstein. On New Year's Eve 2008, after clients sought to withdraw 38% of the fund's capital, the fund stealthily floated a plan to merge its $1.2 billion Steel Partners II fund into a $40 million Pink Sheet Utah loan company.[2]

Like many other activist funds, Steel Partners II makes concentrated investments in companies where it believes it can push for changes that will boost the value of its shares. This strategy worked well for Steel for years, generating returns in excess of 22% between 1993 and 2007. The year 2008, however, was a different story. The combination of sharp declines in equity prices and large, illiquid investments led to a loss of 39% for the year.[3]

Redemption requests came pouring in, eventually totaling approximately $450 million. In order to buy some time and develop a longer-term plan, Lichtenstein decided to suspend all investor redemptions. However, unlike most other funds in similar situations, he put in motion a plan that would reorganize the fund by merging it with an unlisted holding company called WebFinancial Corporation, thereby permanently locking up investor capital. One can imagine the dismayed reaction of shareholders, who had already suffered deep losses and a litany of gates, suspensions, and other restructurings elsewhere in their portfolios.

In his December 31 letter to shareholders, Lichtenstein described both the problem he faced and the merits of the solution he was proposing. His problem, now familiar, was essentially long-term assets and short-term, unstable capital:

> The assets in our model are the businesses, securities, or assets we invest in and the liabilities are created by the quarterly or annual liquidity provisions that give our Partners the ability to withdraw capital prior to the completion of an investment cycle. Clearly, stable capital is needed to successfully carry out our mission and for our Partners to realize the inherent value in our portfolio. The current structure severely limits our ability to successfully execute our investment strategy. It also negatively impacts those investors who have invested in the Partnership long term.

In order to solve these problems, he needed to create a plan that he felt treated all shareholders alike, whether they chose to stay or go.

Lichtenstein outlined this goal while describing the objectives of the plan in his letter:

> Treat all shareholders fairly and equally. Maximize value of the portfolio for all. Provide liquidity for those who have requested it. Fix the mismatch of liquidity terms to match our investment horizon. Retain management to maximize the value of our portfolio companies. Insure proper governance and align compensation with performance.

He went on to say that the fund had considered a variety of solutions that would meet these objectives, including full and partial cash redemptions, distributions in kind, a full liquidation, liquidating trusts, side pockets, dual share classes, and others. In the end, Lichtenstein believed that the merger with WebFinancial was the best alternative to achieve his stated objectives. He ended the letter with a quotation from Mary Kay Ash, the founder of Mary Kay Cosmetics: "Life is full of stumbling blocks or stepping-stones. It all depends on which you choose, one you win and one you lose."

Many investors weren't buying it, and unfortunately for Lichtenstein, one was a shareholder whom you piss off at your peril: Carl Icahn. With an affiliated entity at Bank of America, Icahn sued, seeking, among other things, the return of its original $15 million investment, the reversal of the New Year's Eve transaction, and the sacking of Lichtenstein.[4]

In the lawsuit, Icahn's attorneys used the Mary Kay reference as an artillery shell:

> Mr. Lichtenstein apparently decided to turn the stumbling blocks of his poor performance and the rampant withdrawals from the fund into a path to perpetual fees and possible other profits by using people who entrusted him with their money as unwilling stepping-stones. He has created a scenario in which he is guaranteed to win and they lose, not only by assuring himself an ongoing stream of fees for many years to come, but by also creating for himself an opportunity to buy their interest in the former fund "on the cheap" in the market. He also particularly made sure that he is the only one who gets to choose whether to win or lose; his investors are being forced into the new scheme whether they like it or not.

On one hand, Steel was trying to do what any fund would love to do: create permanent equity capital against long-dated investments. No one could argue with this objective. The timing and method of the proposal, however, couldn't have been worse.

In an environment where structured transactions were wildly out of favor, cash was frustratingly hard to get, and market liquidity had seized up, Steel's plan, illogically, sailed directly into each of these storms. It took a traditional hedge fund structure and backed it into an unlisted holding company with no access to cash except through the sale of shares that currently have no liquidity.

Meanwhile, some investors feared that whenever they ended up with their new WebFinancial shares, they would take a bath. With little or no current liquidity in the shares, they envisioned receiving bids well below their current value. Even worse, if no other investors were willing to bid for the shares, it certainly seemed possible that Steel would step in and buy them out at an even steeper discount.

For many, nothing was more frustrating than the apparent lack of shareholder consultation before the merger. In most funds, any major restructuring requires a shareholder vote. Here, despite the investor letter's claim that the transaction was subject to "confirmation by the Master Fund on or before June 30, 2009," it was unclear to many investors that a vote would take place. Furthermore, Icahn's suit alleged that the plan included a hike in management fees, from between 1% and 1.5% to 2%. If true, this would be particularly grating for those opposed to the plan.

In theory, the attempt to match asset and liability duration made sense. Practically, however, its timing was bad, and the probability of success was low, especially for the goal of a quick return of investor capital. In May 2009, in the face of mounting opposition, Steel offered investors an alternative plan. In this iteration, investors were given the choice to either proceed with the first plan and convert into the listed WebFinancial shares or elect to receive a pro rata distribution of the company's assets.[5] In this option, any investor who chose not to convert into the new listed shares would receive

a direct pro rata portion of each of the company's investments. The responsibility for liquidating these assets would then be borne individually by each investor. For some, the potentially chaotic nature of such an ad hoc liquidation probably seemed even worse than owning shares of WebFinancial. In July 2009, the fund announced that 64% of investors in Steel Partners II voted to become holders of the new publicly traded entity. It remained unclear at the time of the announcement whether Mr. Icahn's lawsuit had been fully resolved. In the end, the fund's long and bruising road to reorganization will likely stand as a reminder of a core hedge fund investor principle: cash is king when a redemption is requested.

A Few Illiquid Exceptions

Before the credit crisis, most investors probably assumed that the assets underlying their hedge fund investments were largely liquid, actively traded securities. In most cases, they were right. The markets for bank debt, high yield, convertible securities, and even CLOs, CDOs, and other asset-backed securities, in general, were frequently traded and could be efficiently bought and sold.

Then came the credit crisis. When the tsunami roared through, $2 to $3 trillion of hedge fund debt and equity capital was washed away; in its wake lay a wreckage of hedge fund assets for sale and almost no new capital of any kind to buy them. The natural result of such an epic imbalance was significantly lower prices and significantly lower liquidity. The lower liquidity was a function of a supply/demand imbalance so wide that the price required to clear it was simply unacceptable to the sellers.

There were a few funds, however, that had kept investments in illiquid securities as a core strategy from the beginning. These funds handled price volatility and capital instability in a very different manner, although they created their own fair share of investor headaches.

D.B. Zwirn & Company

D.B. Zwirn & Company was one of the most controversial of this lot. The firm was started in October 2001 by Dan Zwirn, a former portfolio manager for Highbridge Capital, and grew rapidly, reaching approximately $5 billion in AUM by 2008.[6] Through its flagship Special Opportunities Fund, it pursued a strategy of private investments in corporate loans, real estate loans, equity securities, derivatives, and other thinly traded assets. The private and therefore illiquid nature of these investments was no secret; it was, in fact, part of the fund's stated strategy. The focus was on small and midsized companies that were often overlooked by the larger commercial lenders like Citigroup and Bank of America. This provided the fund with an advantage: with fewer banks targeting the market for small and unconventional loans, Zwirn could create uniquely tailored structures that better met the borrower's objectives while realizing a higher rate of return for the fund.

Target companies for this strategy were often private, nondescript issuers for whom Zwirn may have been the only deal in town. Some of his deals included a $19 million secured loan to Everything But Water, a retailer of women's swimwear; a $15.6 million secured loan to Dorado Beckville Partners, an oil and natural gas exploration and production company in Texas with just 11 wells; a $6 million senior credit facility for Audio Messaging Solutions; and a loan to JHT Holdings, a hauler of new diesel trucks. Zwirn also made many small private equity investments, including a reported 15 "PIPEs" (private investments in public equity) between 2004 and 2006 that averaged less than $5 million each.[7]

Given the time and complexity associated with originating, processing, and monitoring hundreds of such small, bespoke loans each year, the fund amassed a network of 15 offices and a global staff of more than 250 people.[8]

It's not hard to see why Zwirn's investments were highly illiquid: they were originated, priced, and structured by Zwirn, so there was little publicly available information or history on either the companies or the investments. Furthermore, even if an interested buyer signed a nondisclosure agreement in order to receive information about a specific investment, it would take weeks to analyze it, plus more time to negotiate an acceptable purchase price—all for just a $5 or $10 million investment.

For most hedge funds or institutional money managers, that would have been far too much trouble for an investment that wouldn't begin to move the needle of their returns. Consequently, with Zwirn's size and extensive infrastructure, it became one of the largest players in this obscure corner of the hedge fund world. Undoubtedly, that's the way Zwirn liked it.

Unlike virtually every other fund manager discussed in this book, Zwirn understood the inherent need to match the duration of his capital with the long-lived illiquid assets he was accumulating. He apparently required clients to agree to a three-year lockup and a 120-day notice period before they could withdraw capital. Furthermore, if funds were unavailable to pay redemption requests, investors would remain in a separate account that would return capital only when the underlying loans were paid off, a process that could take several years.[9]

As you might expect, during the boom years, the strategy worked well, delivering a steady 1% to 2% a month and annual returns of 15.6% in 2006[10] and 11% in 2007.[11] Like many other funds discussed in this book, Zwirn's consistent, low volatility returns were a magnet for new institutional capital, ensuring a steady flow of new money.

As Zwirn's AUM grew, its portfolio of small, illiquid loans undoubtedly grew as well, probably totaling hundreds of individual investments. Because there was no active secondary market for the loans and little comparable market data to use when preparing monthly marks, Zwirn used its own models to estimate the value of many of its loans.[12] Judging by the consistency of the fund's returns over time, the prices of these loans exhibited relatively little volatility.

The obvious question for any fund using a model to price a large portfolio of small, illiquid, and hard-to-value securities involves the accuracy of that model. For years, the fund ran smoothly, and if there were any concerns about valuation procedures, they were generally answered by clean audits from PricewaterhouseCoopers.

However, storm clouds began to gather in early 2007 when the fund disclosed that an internal investigation had uncovered improper money transfers between funds and expenses that were inappropriately charged to investors. Although the firm paid investors back with interest, the episode coincided with the departure of the fund's CFO and, a short while later, an SEC probe[13] that sent new tremors through the investor network.

Making matters worse, it took until December 2007 for PricewaterhouseCoopers to sign off on Zwirn's financial statements, a remarkably long time for any audit and an eternity for an already rattled investor base.

Attempting to address these problems, Zwirn improved its policies and procedures, hired additional staff, and brought in people who could help to reestablish credibility, including Sandy Berger, U.S. national security advisor under Bill Clinton, and Warren Rudman, former U.S. senator from New Hampshire.

But the bad news kept coming. In 2007, another review by the fund reportedly concluded that a fund manager who'd left in 2005 had failed to "follow a systematic pricing methodology" for a portfolio of high-yield bonds. The firm said its lawyers and auditors uncovered "no conclusive evidence that the portfolio was overvalued" but found that by using one pricing methodology, "the portfolio may have been marginally overvalued." In the spring of 2008, the fund told its investors it had received subpoenas from the SEC seeking information about how the fund valued assets, among other issues.[14]

For investors in a fund with a large proportion of its assets in small, hard-to-value, illiquid loans, this may have been the last straw. Before long, redemptions at Zwirn had ballooned to more than $2 billion, forcing the firm to effectively close the fund. A letter to investors described its assets as "a highly diverse portfolio of illiquid investments in multiple countries." The letter also informed investors that it might take as many as *four* years to wind down the funds.

Unlike almost any other fund manager in a similar situation, Zwirn did not use a gate, suspension, or restructuring. Nor did he

initially attempt to sell the portfolio through an auction or orga-
nized sale. No, he simply told investors: you will get your money
when the loans mature or otherwise pay off—whenever that is.

For many investors, a four-year wind-down period may have
been even more painful than any gate, suspension, or other restructuring they had previously experienced. Moreover, whenever a
hedge fund winds down, maintaining a talented staff of investment
professionals is a notoriously difficult task. For Zwirn investors, this
hurdle was even higher. Given the four-year time horizon and the
size and complexity of the portfolio, maintaining anything less
than a highly skilled and experienced team to oversee the fund
could very quickly compound investor misery.

In April 2009, after a year of managing the liquidation himself,
Zwirn agreed to turn the job over to Fortress Investment Group
LLC. Bloomberg reported at the time that Fortress would be reim-
bursed for the costs of the wind down plus additional compensation
equal to 1% of the fund's net assets and 5% of any profit it makes.
For investors, this addressed the question of staffing during the liquidation by aligning the fund with an established, institutional-
quality hedge fund manager.

The Zwirn situation highlights yet another challenge of illiquid
assets. By definition, there is no market price for the assets, either
because there is not enough information for buyers to make an
informed investment decision or because the market simply can't
agree on the appropriate price. Either way, determining the
monthly value of the assets must be left to the investment manager.
With a large number of unique assets that defy traditional valuation techniques, valuation becomes a very real risk that the investor
must bear.

What Price Risk?

If the fates of Zwirn, Sowood, Amaranth, and Bear have taught investors anything, it may be that the consequences of illiquidity and unstable capital—overnight collapses, gates, suspensions, restructurings, lawsuits, valuation uncertainty, and wind downs— represent a very costly but identifiable risk. As with any risk, there is a set price investors will pay to assume it. For smart investors, however, the future price of this risk in hedge fund investments will be very high indeed.

seven

FRAUD

During the hedge fund golden years, there was no shortage of reports ballyhooing the rarity of fraud in the industry. Despite a lack of any real regulation at the state or federal level, few industry governance standards, and the enormous scope of potential investments—public, private, cash, derivative, foreign, domestic, etc.—fraud, they said, almost never happened. With so many experienced investment professionals performing in-depth due diligence, it would be hard to maintain a fraud for very long, they argued.

Even the Alternative Investment Management Association (AIMA), a leading hedge fund trade association, published a chart in November 2008 (see Figure 7-1) that compared large corporate frauds to losses from hedge fund investments, but it didn't chart an actual hedge fund fraud—almost as if they never occurred.

And then, just a month after this chart was published, everything changed. Bernie Madoff admitted to an incomprehensible, 20-year, $65 billion fraud that dwarfed every other hedge fund or corporate collapse with the exception of WorldCom.

In the wake of the scandal, some in the industry tried to distance themselves from Madoff by arguing that his investment

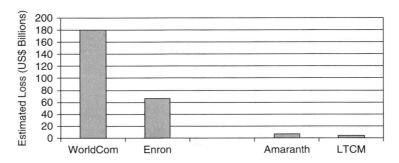

Figure 7-1   Large losses with stocks and hedge funds
Source: Alternative Investment Management Association (AIMA)

vehicle wasn't technically structured like a traditional hedge fund (more on this later). In reality, Madoff was an alternative investment—it was a private vehicle, it pursued a hedged equity strategy, and its largest investors were funds of hedge funds. Consequently, hedge fund investors had to confront a new and even more chilling reality. The investment losses of 2008 were bad, the freeze of investor capital through gates and suspension was worse, but now they were forced to question whether their capital had, in fact, been legitimately invested. For many, the trust that had been built over the course of decades disappeared in an instant.

And there were other scandals, too, including a seven-year, $450 million fraud at the Bayou Group; allegations of false and misleading investor communication against two hedge fund managers at Bear Stearns in the aftermath of its collapse; and a $700 million fraud by lawyer Marc Dreier that ensnared many hedge funds, to name a few.

Fraud 101

In many cases of major hedge fund fraud, the design of the schemes is surprisingly similar. The majority rely on three key practices to eliminate much of the external contact or examination that could expose the scam. They include self-administration, unknown, understaffed, or sham auditors, and internal custody and trade execution of securities. Much like "gentlemen's clubs," these methods of administration can make a fund windowless, so nosy outsiders find it difficult see what's going on inside.

Self-Administration

The vast majority of hedge funds use an independent firm, known as a third-party administrator, to prepare and maintain their accounting records. This function, when performed by an industry leader such as Citco or State Street, is arguably one of the most important deterrents to fraud. Why? Because the process of accurately and independently preparing the books and records of a fund requires near total transparency of the underlying investments. The administrator must independently price all of the fund's investments using publicly recognized pricing sources (or models, if necessary), calculate all interest and dividend accruals, and incorporate any sources of leverage. With this data, the administrator then calculates the NAV of the fund, including all fees and income accruals. Finally, the administrator independently prepares and sends monthly statements to investors.

Now imagine the potential for trouble if a hedge fund performed this function internally, without the assistance or checks of an outside firm. This is known in the industry as self-administration. A self-administrated fund is responsible for pricing all of its own investments—publicly traded, private, or illiquid. Any discretion in this process is theirs and theirs alone. The fund then uses this pricing data to prepare its own financial records and periodic investor statements. The only external check on the fund's pricing data comes in the form of spot checks by its year-end auditor. With so many opportunities for conflict, self-administration has, in a few cases, provided a convenient front for scammers who conduct no legitimate investment activity at all.

It's hard to believe anyone would entrust billions of dollars to a fund that runs its operations this way, but it happens. In light of recent scandals, though, most investors will have a significantly lower appetite for funds that self-administrate.

Unknown Auditors

The role of a fund's auditor is fairly straightforward: the auditor reviews the fund's financial statements at the end of each year to determine if they conform to generally accepted accounting principles (GAAP). In practice, however, the auditor's job is quite difficult, requiring months of painstaking diligence by the audit firm. Done right, the service can provide an excellent check on investment performance, asset verification, process controls, and, ultimately, the overall legitimacy of a fund's activities. Given the importance of this process, any sizable fund should employ a nationally recognized audit firm: Ernst and Young, Deloitte & Touche, PricewaterhouseCoopers, etc. When a fund turns to an unknown or thinly staffed auditor, or a three-man accounting firm, or the founder's Uncle Vinny—well, you get the picture.

Trade Execution and Custody through an Internal Broker-Dealer

The vast majority of hedge funds trade and custody (physically hold for safe keeping) their securities with one or more prime brokers, banks, or other broker-dealers. At the end of each month, the fund gets a statement from the bank or broker-dealer that attests to the existence of the securities, reports the market price, and provides time and price for each trade in the account. This data then becomes another important check on the existence of assets, verification of trade and price activity, and history of the fund's investment activity. Importantly, the use of an external broker-dealer also creates street relationships that can attest to the volumes traded and strategies pursued.

If a fund has its own broker-dealer, it can then custody and settle trades with itself. This leaves the internal broker-dealer in charge of producing the records that attest to the physical existence of securities or other assets within the fund and any trading activity that takes place on its behalf. By self-producing these records, a fund eliminates another important element of third-party verification. For a hedge fund manager intent on committing a fraud, fabricated records from an internal broker-dealer can help to conceal both missing assets and the absence of an extensive series of Wall Street trading relationships that would otherwise naturally exist for a multibillion-dollar fund.

When fraudulent custody and trading records from an internal broker-dealer are combined with sham customer statements produced through self-administration, and each are blessed by a complicit accountant, all records regarding the existence, trading activity, and performance of the assets are internally controlled. In this vacuum, a Ponzi scheme or other hedge fund fraud can be sustained for years.

The Mother of All Frauds: Bernie Madoff

He was Wall Street's elder statesman, a former chairman of the NASDAQ stock exchange. His firm traded as much as 5% of the volume on the New York Stock Exchange. His investment advisory business was so exclusive that access to the fund was often on an invitation-only basis. His clients were the A list of major business leaders, Hollywood stars, and leading universities and endowments. His reputation in business and society was, in short, impeccable.

And yet, on December 10, 2008, Bernie Madoff, chairman of Madoff Securities, told his sons, Andrew and Mark, that he was "finished." His investment advisory business was "one big lie." The sons called the authorities, and the following day the FBI arrested Madoff and charged him with securities fraud.

After his arrest, Madoff admitted to federal authorities that there was "no innocent explanation," that he had "paid people with money that wasn't there and was insolvent," and, shockingly, he said he had "liabilities of approximately $50 billion." Investigators would later discover that he actually had accounts representing the extraordinary sum of $65 billion from pensions, foundations, endowments, FOFs, and high net worth investors. Nearly the entire amount was effectively lost or paid out in what turned out to be the largest Ponzi scheme ever.

Bernard Lawrence "Bernie" Madoff was born in Queens, New York, attended Far Rockaway High School, and graduated from Hofstra University in 1960 with a degree in political science. He reportedly started Madoff Securities in 1960 with just $5,000 in personal savings. Initially, the firm made markets in small capitalization stocks that were traded on the National Quotation Bureau's "Pink Sheets." Over time, the firm developed a technology that allowed it to advertise bid-offer prices more broadly and therefore compete more effectively with the New York Stock Exchange's traditional "open cry" auction system, where buyers and sellers gather on the floor of the exchange to shout buy and sell orders.

Ultimately, this technology worked so well that it contributed significantly to what is now the NASDAQ electronic exchange. As a pioneer in electronic trading, Madoff made himself into one of the largest traders on Wall Street, handling up to 5% of the trading volume on the New York Stock Exchange by the mid 1980s. With this success came prestige; Madoff quickly became one of the most prominent players on Wall Street. In addition to chairing the board of directors of the NASDAQ exchange, he was a member of the NASD (the National Association of Securities Dealers, an industry regulatory body), sat on numerous NASD committees, and was a founding member of the International Securities Clearing Corporation.

This blue-chip pedigree so gilded Madoff's reputation that his integrity was virtually beyond reproach. Why, then, did this industry leader with a highly successful, legitimate broker-dealer business squander his accomplishments in a Ponzi scheme—particularly when such schemes inevitably result in collapse and incarceration? Madoff has yet to offer an explanation, and we may never know. What is clear, though, is that Madoff's sterling street reputation was a magnet for capital in his investment advisory business. If you had to trust someone in the Wild West hedge fund world of the 1980s, who better than the former chairman of the stock exchange?

The following excerpt from Madoff's Web site shows how his reputation as industry patriarch was marketed and how the pitch fostered the critical element of the fraud's success: trust.

The Owner's Name Is on the Door

In an era of faceless organizations owned by other equally faceless organizations, Bernard L. Madoff Investment Securities LLC harks back to an earlier era in the financial world: The owner's name is on the door. Clients know that Bernard Madoff has a personal interest in maintaining the unblemished record of value, fair-dealing, and high ethical standards that has always been the firm's hallmark.

Bernard L. Madoff founded the investment firm that bears his name in 1960, soon after leaving law school. His brother, Peter B. Madoff, graduated from law school and joined the firm in 1970. While building the firm into a significant force in the securities industry, they have both been deeply involved in leading the dramatic transformation that has been underway in U.S. securities trading.

Bernard L. Madoff has been a major figure in the National Association of Securities Dealers (NASD), the major self-regulatory organization for US broker-dealer firms. The firm was one of the five broker-dealers most closely involved in developing the NASDAQ Stock Market. He has been chairman of the board of directors of the NASDAQ Stock Market as well as a member of the board of governors of the NASD and a member of numerous NASD committees.

One major U.S. financial publication lauded Bernard Madoff for his role in "helping to make NASDAQ a faster, fairer, more efficient, and more international system." He has also served as a member of the board of directors of the Securities Industry Association.

The Returns: Perfection, for Nearly Two Decades

For institutional investors seeking to meet internal asset growth targets, the ideal hedge fund investment delivers on three highly

Table 7-1 Annual Returns for Fairfield Sentry Limited, the Largest Madoff Feeder Fund

1990	1991	1992	1993	1994	1995	1996	1997	1998	1999
2.83	18.58	14.67	11.68	11.49	12.95	12.99	14.00	13.40	14.18

2000	2001	2002	2003	2004	2005	2006	2007	2008
11.55	10.68	9.33	8.21	7.07	2.52	9.50	7.34	4.40

coveted objectives: (1) mid-double-digit net returns, (2) low volatility, and (3) returns that are uncorrelated to the stock and bond markets.

Madoff's returns met these objectives with unwavering precision year after year. Table 7-1 shows the annual returns as recorded by the largest Madoff feeder fund, Fairfield Sentry Limited, whose core investment (at least 95%) was Madoff's fund.[1] These returns are net of the 1% management fee and 20% performance fee that Fairfield Greenwich charged its investors.

A quick examination of the feeder fund's other stats underscores the level of perfection achieved in Madoff's reported returns. Table 7-2 highlights how each of the three key investor objectives were met with extraordinary consistency over nearly two decades:

Table 7-2 Key Performance Statistics

Average annual return	11.40%
Average monthly return	0.90%
Percentage of months profitable	95%
Longest losing streak	1 month
Monthly standard deviation (Vol.)	0.7%
Beta	0.06

Source: Key investment statistics derived from analyzing the monthly returns of the largest Madoff feeder fund, Fairfield Sentry, Ltd.

11.40% average annual returns; a Beta, or correlation to the market, of just 0.06; and monthly volatility of only 0.75%.

The Structure of the Fund

From the beginning, Madoff's fund was different from most other hedge funds; in fact, it was not even structured like a traditional hedge fund. Instead, investors understood that it was run as a trading strategy out of Madoff's own internal broker-dealer, which was designed to generate investment returns free of the traditional 2% and 20% hedge fund management and underwriting fees. Madoff told investors that his firm made money by charging commissions on the stock and option trades the firm did on their behalf. Like many other aspects of Madoff's operation, this arrangement, in hindsight, seems almost too good to be true. With an average of $25 billion under management, if Madoff had used a traditional 2% and 20% fee structure, his returns would have produced annual fees of close to $1 billion for the firm. Even assuming generous stock commissions of four cents a share, fees generated under the Madoff commission structure would have represented only a fraction of those available to other hedge funds—particularly suspicious for a fund generating such exceptionally attractive, market leading returns.

Instead of the traditional master-feeder hedge fund structure (which provides investors with a direct partnership interest in the fund), Madoff required investors to open discretionary accounts at his securities firm, which delegated full trading authority for the portfolios to Madoff and his team. Because a number of these discretionary accounts belonged to feeder funds that provided exclusive access, many investors had to rely on their feeder fund for any due diligence performed on the primary Madoff fund — another key to controlling the fraud.

The "Split Strike" Myth

According to Madoff's court confession, for nearly two decades, he did not make any legitimate investments in the fund. Instead, he simply paid out investment returns and redemption requests with newly raised, incoming cash. To help cover the scheme, Madoff told investors that a single investment strategy, known as the "split strike conversion," which involved trading stocks and listed stock options, covered all of the fund's investment capital. Unlike many of the other hedge fund strategies described in this book, the split strike is well known but generally not pursued by other funds. It would be fair to say that few, if any, managers have ever been able to generate attractive returns using the split strike. Like many other liquid, exchange-driven markets, the listed options market rarely offers a free lunch. And in the case of a split strike strategy, it is not even clear if the crumbs from lunch are there for the taking.

A split strike is supposed to work like this: The fund begins by purchasing between 30 and 40 large capitalization stocks such as GE, IBM, McDonald's, etc. It then simultaneously buys out-of-the-money put options and sells out-of-the-money call options on a large cap index such as the S&P 100. Given that many of the stocks in the fund's portfolio are also members of the S&P 100, the correlation between the portfolio and the index should be high. The number of calls and puts that are bought and sold each represent a dollar amount that is roughly equal to the value of the fund's stock portfolio.

The purpose of the put options is to limit the downside in the portfolio of stocks. By purchasing a put option, Madoff would have been purchasing insurance. If the index price trades lower than the strike price of the put option, the buyer is paid the difference between the strike price and the market price of the index at the maturity of the option. The sale of call options, on the other hand, has the effect of both generating income (through the premium received upon the sale of the option) to offset some of the cost of the put options and, at the same time, limiting the potential upside in the portfolio by giving away (to the buyer of the call option) any upside in the index beyond the call strike price.

Taken together, the economics of this series of positions would seem to produce very little in the way of excess returns. Typically, a 10% out-of-the-money put option on any stock or index will cost a few percentage points per year more than a 10% out-of-the-money call option. Today, a one year, 10% out-of-the-money S&P 100 index put option would cost approximately 10% to 12% of the value of the underlying shares. A one year, 10% out-of-the-money S&P 100 index call option, if sold against the fund's portfolio, would generate only 7% to 9% of the underlying shares in sale proceeds. Thus, the option strategy is likely to produce a net *cost* to the fund of roughly 3% a year.

If one then assumes that the dividend income on the stock portfolio produced a gain of roughly 3% annually, then before the gains achieved from stock picking, the net return of the fund is close to zero. This means that the fund needed to generate all of its returns, which averaged around 12% a year, from trading its portfolio of 30 to 40 highly liquid, efficiently valued common stocks, with the upside of the portfolio capped at roughly 10%.

Furthermore, Madoff claimed that he frequently traded in and out of the markets, maintaining exposure to equities only for a fraction of the year. The likelihood of achieving his returns under these constraints in any single year is exceptionally low; doing so for decades would be all but impossible. You'd just as soon expect Derek Jeter to bat .900 every year, for his entire career. Of the many red flags raised by Madoff's methods, this was one of the more obvious.

An even more glaring issue was the absence of open interest in the S&P 100 index options that even approached the size Madoff would have needed to hedge a $25 to $50 billion portfolio. Total open interest in S&P 100 call and put options rarely exceeds a notional value of $10 billion. This creates a gaping hole that the fund would have had to fill in the over-the-counter market. It seems equally unlikely that any bank or group of banks would have wanted that level of exposure to a single fund. Furthermore, if the fund invested $25 to $50 billion in an (unlevered) portfolio of 35 stocks, it would have had to own roughly $1 billion of exposure in each position—an amount that would have made Madoff one of the largest shareholders in 35% of the stocks in the S&P 100.

Inexplicably, he never appeared as a significant owner in any of the stocks. Madoff apparently deflected questions about this by suggesting that he sold all of his positions just prior to quarter end to avoid SEC reporting requirements. Here again, a quarter-end review of trading volumes for S&P 100 companies doesn't support his explanation.

Too Good to Be True

As defined by Madoff, the split strike conversion was in essence a long stock strategy with an option overlay that allowed gains and losses within a window of price movements. Given this definition, any investor looking at the monthly return data must have been truly astounded. Of the 215 months of Madoff feeder fund performance data in Table 7-3, only 10 months are negative. Incredibly, the other 95% are flat or positive. This rate of success is all the more striking if you compare the fund's returns (shown in Figure 7-2) against certain periods when the performance of the S&P 100 was sharply negative.

September 2001 comes immediately to mind. The S&P 100 declined 7.7% in the wake of the terrorist attacks. Fairfield Sentry's Madoff feeder fund? Up 73 basis points. How about the recession and dot-com crash of 2000 to 2002? From January 1, 2000, to December 31, 2002, the S&P 100 declined 44%. The feeder fund managed to record a cumulative gain of 35% with just one down month. To call such performance implausible would be an understatement.

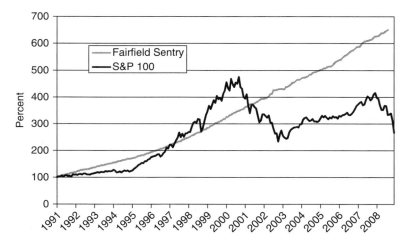

Figure 7-2 Historical Madoff returns vs. the S&P 100

Table 7-3 Fairfield Sentry Limited (Madoff Feeder Fund) Monthly Performance, 1990 to 2008

	Jan	Feb	Mar	Apr	May	Jun	Jul	Aug	Sep	Oct	Nov	Dec	Annual
1990												2.8%	2.8%
1991	3.1%	1.5%	0.6%	1.4%	1.9%	0.4%	2.0%	1.1%	0.8%	2.8%	0.1%	1.6%	18.6%
1992	0.5%	2.8%	1.0%	2.9%	−0.2%	1.3%	0.0%	0.9%	0.4%	1.4%	1.4%	1.4%	14.7%
1993	0.0%	1.9%	1.9%	0.1%	1.7%	0.9%	0.1%	1.8%	0.4%	1.8%	0.3%	0.5%	11.7%
1994	2.2%	−0.4%	1.5%	1.8%	0.5%	0.3%	1.8%	0.4%	0.8%	1.9%	−0.6%	0.7%	11.5%
1995	0.9%	0.8%	0.8%	1.7%	1.7%	0.5%	1.1%	−0.2%	1.7%	1.6%	0.5%	1.1%	13.0%
1996	1.5%	0.7%	1.2%	0.6%	1.4%	0.2%	1.9%	0.3%	1.2%	1.1%	1.6%	0.5%	13.0%
1997	2.5%	0.7%	0.9%	1.2%	0.6%	1.3%	0.8%	0.4%	2.4%	0.6%	1.6%	0.4%	14.0%
1998	0.9%	1.3%	1.8%	0.4%	1.8%	1.3%	0.8%	0.3%	1.0%	1.9%	0.8%	0.3%	13.4%
1999	2.1%	0.2%	2.3%	0.4%	1.5%	1.8%	0.4%	0.9%	0.7%	1.1%	1.6%	0.4%	14.2%
2000	2.2%	0.2%	1.8%	0.3%	1.4%	0.8%	0.7%	1.3%	0.3%	0.9%	0.7%	0.4%	11.5%
2001	2.2%	0.1%	1.1%	1.3%	0.3%	0.2%	0.4%	1.0%	0.7%	1.3%	1.2%	0.2%	10.7%
2002	0.0%	0.6%	0.5%	1.2%	2.1%	0.3%	3.4%	−0.1%	0.1%	0.7%	0.2%	0.1%	9.3%
2003	−0.3%	0.0%	2.0%	0.1%	1.0%	1.0%	1.4%	0.2%	0.9%	1.3%	−0.1%	0.3%	8.2%
2004	0.9%	0.5%	0.1%	0.4%	0.7%	1.3%	0.1%	1.3%	0.5%	0.0%	0.8%	0.2%	7.1%
2005	0.5%	0.4%	0.9%	0.1%	0.6%	0.5%	0.1%	0.2%	0.9%	1.6%	0.8%	0.5%	7.3%
2006	0.7%	0.2%	1.3%	0.9%	0.7%	0.5%	1.1%	0.8%	0.7%	0.4%	0.9%	0.9%	9.5%
2007	0.3%	−0.1%	1.6%	1.0%	0.8%	0.2%	0.2%	0.3%	0.2%	0.5%	1.0%	0.2%	6.4%
2008	0.6%	0.1%	0.2%	0.9%	0.8%	−0.1%	0.7%	0.7%	0.5%	−0.1%			4.4%

Marketing the Fund

For nearly two decades, Madoff was able to raise money with ease. As years passed, his growing track record of extraordinarily steady, uncorrelated, midteen returns attracted institutional and high net worth investors alike. For many years, the fund was closed to outside investors. To get in, an investor needed a "connection" to Bernie or simply had to wait until the fund opened to new capital again. With this aura of exclusivity and a multidecade track record, Madoff established a truly global marketing network, attracting a remarkably diverse group of investors from major FOFs, pension plans, university endowments, smaller charities, foundations, and many notable wealthy individuals, among them actor Kevin Bacon, founder of Nine West Jerome Fisher, and French heiress Liliane Bettencourt.

Madoff's deception seemed to know no bounds as it ensnared friends, business associates, country club golf pals, and relatives alike. In the early days, he relied heavily on his connections in the Jewish communities of New York and Palm Beach. Over time, however, as the fraud grew larger, he began to utilize feeder funds created by the Fairfield Greenwich Group, the Tremont Group, and others.

The Feeder Funds

The feeder funds served Madoff in two critical ways. First, they expanded his marketing reach to the four corners of the globe and helped raise the exponential sums of capital needed to sustain the scheme. Second, they provided a due diligence buffer that helped to limit the number of parties that could investigate the fund.

Recall that Madoff required investors to open discretionary accounts at his securities firm that granted him ultimate authority over the portfolios. By granting discretionary account access to a limited number of investors, Madoff could channel a significant portion of his capital through the feeder funds and reduce the sources of due diligence inquiry.

From a marketing perspective, the feeders were wildly successful. Spurred on by massive fees, the Fairfield Greenwich Group and Tremont Group, the two largest feeders, together raised close to $11 billion.

Fairfield Greenwich Group

The Fairfield Greenwich Group's Fairfield Sentry Limited Fund was by far the largest of the feeder funds. In business since 1990, it had grown to approximately $7.5 billion, nearly twice the bulk of the Tremont Group's fund. At that size, with fees of 1% of assets and 20% of Madoff's performance, the Sentry fund had the potential to generate more than $150 million in fees for Fairfield Greenwich per year—an extraordinary sum for a fund that provided effectively two services: due diligence and access.

To achieve such massive growth in AUM, Fairfield Greenwich aggressively marketed the low volatility, consistently positive return profile of the fund as golden fruit before investors. A remarkable edition of Fairfield Greenwich's semiannual newsletter for the Sentry fund appeared in February 2008. After years of secrecy surrounding Madoff and his strategy, the newsletter attempted a detailed explanation of how the split strike conversion strategy worked, complete with several graphs to drive home the key marketing points of consistency and low risk:

As many of our investors know, Sentry applies a synthetic index replicator and options trading strategy known as the split strike conversion ("SSC") and alternates between periods of time invested in this combined stock/options position and time invested in a cash stance consisting of short dated U.S. Treasury Bills. As such, the fund typically spends more than half of the trading days in each year exposed to movements in the S&P 100 Index, albeit on a hedged basis. For the rest of the year, the fund assumes a "risk free" Treasury position and earns short-term money market rates of return as it seeks to protect capital during unfavorable market conditions for the SSC.

The key to switching between these stances boils down to a question of timing—and timing, in its various forms, is the principal source of alpha in this strategy.

In essence, Fairfield Greenwich was telling investors that Madoff's extraordinary success emanated from an almost mystical ability to simply ride the up markets and sit out the bad markets. The newsletter went on to explain that Madoff was typically invested in equities for just one or two months at a time:

As one might expect, consistently delivering positive performance across different market environments requires some adaptation. Bull markets of the sort seen in the later 1990s (and even as recently as 2006) are ripe with entry and exit opportunities conducive to bull spread investing. Conversely, bear markets characterized by negative momentum, skittish investor behavior, and poor liquidity pose additional timing and trading challenges. Over the 17 years it has been in existence, Sentry has recognized and adapted to a number of these regime shifts.

For example, in the momentum and liquidity rich equity markets of 2006, Sentry accurately identified four major trend reversals during the year and implemented the SSC strategy around these periods of positive market directionality. Each of these four implementations lasted more than two months (longer than its long-run average holding of four weeks). In contrast, weaker equity markets in 2007, characterized by relatively fewer periods of sustained positive market directionality (especially during the latter half of the year), meant that trading had to be more nimble and the SSC had to be constructed around shorter-term perceived trading opportunities. In fact, of the seven implementation cycles in 2007, all but one lasted fewer than four weeks.

For the sake of argument, let's say the letter convinced at least some investors that 17 straight years of perfect returns were all due to Madoff's godlike market-timing capabilities. Even so, the idea that Madoff bought and sold $50 billion worth of stocks multiple times a year must have been hard for many to swallow. To accept this assertion, one would have to believe that Madoff traded hundreds of billions of dollars annually in just the 100 stocks of the S&P 100 without ever appearing in 13F ownership records or affecting the trading of any of the shares.

An equally remarkable analysis contained in the newsletter provided a highly detailed, to-the-basis-point (1/100 of a percent) calculation that explained the attribution of 2007 profit and loss between the options profit and loss, stock dividends, T-bill interest, and stock trading profit and loss (see Table 7-4).

Upon close examination, Table 7-4 reveals two extraordinary feats of investment skill. First, it shows that in 2007 the fund earned 3.82% in its stock portfolio, roughly the same return as the

Table 7-4 2007 Approximate Profit and Loss Attribution by Instrument Type of Split Strike Conversion Assets

	Stock P&L	T-Bill Interest	Net Dividends	Options P&L	Net Profit
Q1 2007	−1.11%	0.56%	0.10%	2.28%	1.82%
Q2 2007	3.38%	0.28%	0.23%	−1.73%	2.14%
Q3 2007	2.09%	0.68%	0.06%	−1.26%	1.45%
Q4 2007	−0.60%	0.64%	0.05%	1.72%	1.74%
2007	3.82%	2.18%	0.43%	0.91%	7.34%

Source: Fairfield Greenwich's February 2008 Sentry Fund newsletter

S&P 100, despite being invested in cash for a substantial part of the year and utilizing option hedges that capped the fund's upside at around 10%. A second magical achievement: getting paid 0.91% on presumably unexercised option hedges throughout the year—a feat not currently possible in the listed options market, where it typically costs more than 2% if the put and call collar hedges are equally out of the money.

Once the newsletter wrapped up its demonstrations of Madoff's prestidigitation, it turned to its true purpose, marketing. Here the message was clear and simple: high returns, low volatility. Enjoy the upside gains available in the equity market with risk not significantly higher than owning U.S. government Treasury bills.

The first two graphs emphasizing this point are highlighted in Figure 7-3. The graphs plot the standard deviation of the fund's performance, a measure of the fund's volatility or risk, and its net performance against the same numbers for the S&P 100 and U.S. government T-bills.

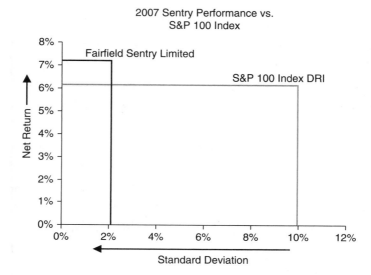

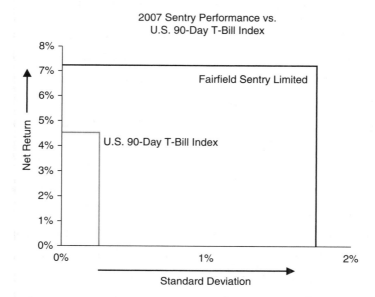

Figure 7-3 Return/volatility charts for the Fairfield Sentry Limited Fund
Source: Fairfield Greenwich's February 2008 Sentry Fund newsletter

The newsletter offered this explanation of the graphs:

As can be seen in [Figure 7-3], over the past year Sentry has delivered a net return of 122 basis points above the S&P 100 index with a fraction of the volatility. Similarly, the fund has exceeded the 90-day Treasury bill rate by 295 basis points. These results are quite intuitive when one considers the bull spread profile of the SSC. The combination of a synthetic index (composed of a basket of stocks designed to replicate the S&P 100 Index) and an options wrapper (consisting of short out-of-the-money S&P 100 Index calls and long out-of-the-money S&P Index puts) means that Sentry is designed to provide large cap U.S. equity exposure within a range, but with much less volatility. Since the inception of the fund in 1990, Sentry's volatility, as measured by a 36 month standard deviation, has ranged between 1.34% and 3.23% and is currently 1.4%.

The pitch, then, was 8% returns with risk comparable to U.S. government securities. An extraordinary multiyear achievement? Not according to the newsletter, which described it as "quite intuitive." Still not sold? Consider the two graphs in Figure 7-4, which compared the performance of Sentry to the five best and worst six-month periods of performance in the S&P 100 index.

Again, in good times and bad, the result was always the same: the fund made money and plenty of it. Given the admitted absence of any real investments in the fund over the preceding 16 years, the detail provided in this newsletter is striking. The to-the-basis-point precision offered by Fairfield Greenwich for attribution between stock gains, T-bill interest, option premium, and detailed market-timing information most likely came from Madoff himself, perhaps an offering of greater "transparency" meant to drive away redemption clouds possibly gathering on the horizon.

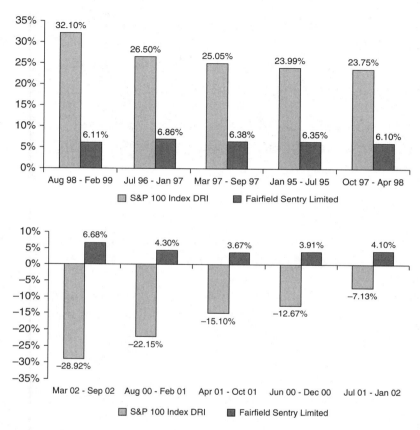

Figure 7-4 Sentry's performance during the best (top) and worst (bottom) six-month periods for the S&P 100 DRI Index
Source: Fairfield Greenwich's February 2008 Sentry Fund newsletter

The Inevitable Lawsuits

Given the capital raised and fees generated by the feeders, it is not surprising that they have been subject to a number of lawsuits. Fairfield Greenwich has been named in several class action investor lawsuits and a suit by the state of Massachusetts over due diligence failures. In these complaints, the plaintiffs have tended to focus on failed due diligence representations allegedly made by Fairfield Greenwich (FGG) in its Private Placement Memorandum and other marketing documents. A few examples of these alleged marketing representations are listed below:[2]

i. FGG would seek "to dissect a candidate manager's investment performance, how they generate alpha, and what risks are taken in doing so";

ii. "Only by receiving full transparency from its managers can FFG assure itself and its clients that every FFG fund continues to act according to the principles, agreements, and strategies, that are specified to FGG and investors"

iii. A "key aspect" to transparency was whether information was "provided by an independent third party—such as a broker-dealer—or by the manager, where it might be subject to manipulation."

In response to the Massachusetts and other suits, Fairfield Greenwich has rejected any allegations of fraud. In a statement it said: "FGG's diligence and risk management practices were consistent with its representations to Sentry investors, and the Sentry Offering Memoranda made clear that Madoff held substantially all of the funds' assets." The response went on to say, "Given FGG's robust monitoring over the course of nearly twenty years, the assertion that FGG failed to conduct diligence in a manner amounting to fraud is entirely inconsistent with the objective facts."

With several hundred million of fees in hand, Fairfield Greenwich and the other feeder funds are a natural target for investors who suffered $65 billion in losses. Whether Fairfield will ultimately be judged another victim of the fraud or as a liable counterparty to the losses remains to be seen.

A final question regarding the feeder funds involves the role of their auditors. Although Madoff's auditor was an obscure, one-man operation also accused of fraud, Fairfield Sentry was audited by nationally recognized PricewaterhouseCoopers. Although it was not explicitly its job to perform a second level audit of underlying fund investments, many observers have suggested that Pricewater- houseCoopers should have spotted more of the red flags. PricewaterhouseCoopers has responded to these questions by saying "PwC Canada provided auditing services to the Fairfield Sentry fund, but was not the auditor for Bernard Madoff Invest- ments where the alleged fraud occurred. PwC Canada's auditing of Fairfield Sentry's financial statements complied with profes- sional standards."[3]

Sadly, the list of victims is a long one, highlighting the scale and efficiency of the marketing machine created by Madoff and the feeder funds.

Table 7-5 Selected List of Madoff Investors

Fairfield Greenwich Group (Madoff feeder fund)	Fund of hedge funds	$7.5 billion
FIM Ltd.	Fund of hedge funds	$3.5 billion
Grupo Santander	Bank	$3.5 billion
Tremont Group (Madoff feeder fund)	Fund of hedge funds	$3.3 billion
Kingate Management	Fund of hedge funds	$2.8 billion
Bank Medici of Austria	Bank	$2.1 billion
Ascot Partners	Fund of hedge funds	$1.8 billion
Access International Advisors	Fund of hedge funds	$1.4 billion

(Continued)

Table 7-5 Selected List of Madoff Investors (*Continued*)

Fortis Bank Nederland	Bank	$1.35 billion
HSBC	Bank	$1 billion
Union Bancaire Privee	Fund of hedge funds	$700 million
Natixis	Bank	$600 million
Royal Bank of Scotland	Bank	$600 million
Ruth and Carl Shapiro	Individuals	$400 million
RMF (Man Group)	Fund of hedge funds	$360 million
Pioneer Alternative Investments	Fund of hedge funds	$280 million
Maxam Capital Management (Madoff feeder fund)	Fund of hedge funds	$280 million
EIM Group	Bank	$230 million
Ira Rennert	Individual	$200 million
Jerome Fisher	Individual, founder of Nine West	$150 million
Carl and Ruth Shapiro Family Foundation	Charity	$145 million
Mortimer B. Zuckerman Charitable Remainder Trust	Charity, owner of N.Y. Daily News	$30 million
Madoff Family Foundation	Charity	$19 million
Los Angeles Jewish Community Foundation	Charity	$18 million
Foundation for Humanity	Elie Wiesel's charity	$15.2 million
Massachusetts Pension Reserves Investment Management	Pension fund	$12 million
New York Law School	Law school	$3 million
Kevin Bacon and Kyra Sedgwick	Individuals, actors	n/a
Norman Braman	Individual, former owner of the Philadelphia Eagles	n/a
Leonard Feinstein	Individual, Bed Bath & Beyond cofounder	n/a
Avram and Carol Goldberg	Individuals, Founders of Stop & Shop	n/a
JEHT Foundation	Charity	n/a

Henry Kaufman	Individual, former chief economist at Salomon Brothers	n/a
Palm Beach Country Club	Country club	n/a
Family of Eliot Spitzer	Individual, former governor of New York State	n/a
Wilpon family	Family office, owner of New York Mets	n/a
Wunderkinder Foundation	Steven Spielberg's charity	n/a

Source: Wall Street Journal

The Classic Warning Signs

Avoiding Madoff's Ponzi scheme required a level of discipline that escaped many individual and even institutional investors. One had to ignore his stellar reputation; dismiss the near perfection of the level, volatility, and beta of his historical returns; and resist the exclusivity of the rich and famous Madoff "club." If, however, an investor could look beyond this glossy marketing pitch and objectively examine the fund from a due diligence perspective, the allure would have diminished significantly. Through this lens, Madoff would have stood out as a poster child for potential hedge fund fraud, incorporating every classic element of bad fund governance and inadequate investor protection. In the end, it was the absence of these controls that enabled the fraud to carry on for nearly 20 years.

The Internal Broker-Dealer

Madoff Securities acted as the broker-dealer for Madoff's investment advisor, an arrangement that enabled two critical elements of the fraud. First, having an internal broker-dealer fill the role of custodian (physical guardian) for securities supposedly purchased by the fund allowed Madoff to create bogus reports attesting to the existence of securities when, in reality, there were none at all. An independent custodian would have reported the actual assets held by the fund and could have exposed the fraud to the fund's auditor (assuming, of course, the auditor was on the level).

Second, by purporting to execute all the fund's trades through his internal broker-dealer, Madoff was able to create fictitious trading records that supported fabricated customer statements and thus avoided the contradicting facts of independent trade reports. Conveniently, having an internal broker-dealer also provided Madoff an easy explanation for why the fund, which should have traded hundreds of millions of shares a year, lacked a significant trading relationship with a major Wall Street firm.

Self-Administration

The Madoff scam demonstrated that, with self-administration, all things are possible. By keeping critical administrative functions intramural, Madoff was able to create, maintain, and control each of the many façades that sustained the fraud. He maintained his own books and records; created and marked his own fictitious investments; calculated his own fees/commissions; determined his own returns; and, finally, created his own monthly statements, which were mailed to investors—all without the pesky questions of any independent administrator. By keeping everyone on the other side of the curtain, the mighty wizard was free to pull the levers and turn the knobs of the machine that wowed investors ever hungry for steady returns.

The Auditor

The firm that audited Bernard L. Madoff Investment Securities and certified that all was accurate, true, and in full compliance with GAAP was a three-person shop called Friehling & Horowitz. Reportedly, the firm operated out of a 13- by 18-foot office in a small strip mall in suburban New York. Legitimate or not, with only one employee—David Friehling—working as an active accountant, the firm was in no way equipped to audit Madoff. One accountant providing an annual audit for a $50+ billion hedge fund will catch about as much malfeasance as one NYPD cop in Times Square on New Year's Eve.

After an investigation by the U.S. Attorney's Office, Friehling was arrested on fraud charges in March 2009 and accused of rubber-stamping Madoff's books for 17 years. Before the authorities moved in, however, it seems that few investors tried to learn much about this tiny, unknown firm with the sole external and presumably independent right to inspect the $65 billion vehicle they were staked in. Had anyone probed Friehling & Horowitz, they would have learned that the firm had been telling the American Institute of Certified Public Accountants for 15 years that it didn't conduct audits.[4] Given the depth of resources at most FOFs and other institutional investors, it is particularly shocking that no one apparently bothered to seriously investigate this small and unknown audit firm. Had a nationally recognized firm such as Ernst & Young or KPMG been the auditor, the Ponzi scheme almost certainly never would have gotten off the ground.

Where Did the Money Go?

In most cases of theft-motivated fraud, the prospect for any meaningful recovery of assets is grim. Often, investor capital is systematically drained away. The cash is used to pay bogus returns to other investors; lavished on mansions, luxury cars, and yachts; distributed to other employees in outsized compensation packages; and larded into charity donations. Once the thieves' den is found, records of the largess either don't exist or are in complete disarray.

Like any good Ponzi man, Madoff dealt all of these cards and more. However, given the scale and duration of his scheme, it appears that the majority of the missing $65 billion was simply paid out to satisfy redemption requests and pay "investment returns." Anything that remained was most likely used to enrich Madoff and other close associates. A short list of Madoff's known assets includes a $23 million Palm Beach mansion, an $8 million New York penthouse, a beachfront estate in Montauk, Long Island, European homes, country club memberships, a 55-foot yacht named Bull, and so on. There is also ample evidence of largess in donations to charities that enhanced his social standing and kept new capital at the ready.

Finding the Cheese

To attempt an accounting of the billions squandered through Madoff's scheme, a few assumptions are necessary. First, one needs to take Madoff at his word and assume that he didn't make any legitimate investments. SEC 13F filings of shareholdings and trading volumes in the stock and option markets seem to support his claim. Next, one needs to make some guesses about the growth of AUM. For the sake of argument, let's assume the AUM was $1 billion in 1990 and grew through a combination of fictitious investment returns and 15% capital growth per year until it finally reached roughly $65 billion in 2008.

Further assume that 15% of the annual bogus Madoff investment "profit" was paid in cash to investors that needed the money to cover living expenses or make required institutional or charity payouts. Finally, assume that, on average, 3% of the fund's AUM was paid out to investors requesting redemption each year and 0.5% was taken by Madoff himself.

On the back of these assumptions, the fund would have paid out a total of $18 billion in cash from 1990 until 2008 including an estimated $2 billion to Madoff himself. Given that Madoff's investment returns were, by his own admission, fictitious, it stands to reason that the actual cash lost by investors will be less than the fund's estimated AUM. The AUM of the fund, which is effectively the $65 billion that has been reported missing, is the sum of cash invested plus the fictitious investment returns. Table 7-6 provides a simplistic calculation of how $18 billion of real investor cash held by the fund may have disappeared. None of the figures have been adjusted to include the time value of money.

Table 7-6 A Hypothetical Account of Lost Madoff Assets

	Estimated Madoff Gross "Investment Returns"	Estimated AUM 15% Capital Growth Plus "Investment Returns" (in billions)	15% Payout of Gross "Returns" (in billions)	Madoff's Take 0.5% of AUM/ Year (in billions)	Redemptions Paid 3% AUM/ Year (in billions)
1990	20%	$1	$0.0	$0.0	$0.0
1991	24%	$1	$0.0	$0.0	$0.0
1992	19%	$2	$0.1	$0.0	$0.1
1993	16%	$2	$0.1	$0.0	$0.1
1994	15%	$3	$0.1	$0.0	$0.1
1995	17%	$4	$0.1	$0.0	$0.1

(Continued)

Table 7-6 A Hypothetical Account of Lost Madoff Assets (*Continued*)

	Estimated Madoff Gross "Investment Returns"	Estimated AUM 15% Capital Growth Plus "Investment Returns" (in billions)	15% Payout of Gross "Returns" (in billions)	Madoff's Take 0.5% of AUM/ Year (in billions)	Redemptions Paid 3% AUM/ Year (in billions)
1996	17%	$5	$0.1	$0.0	$0.1
1997	18%	$6	$0.2	$0.0	$0.2
1998	18%	$8	$0.2	$0.0	$0.2
1999	19%	$10	$0.3	$0.1	$0.3
2000	15%	$13	$0.3	$0.1	$0.4
2001	14%	$16	$0.4	$0.1	$0.5
2002	13%	$20	$0.4	$0.1	$0.6
2003	11%	$25	$0.4	$0.1	$0.8
2004	10%	$30	$0.4	$0.2	$0.9
2005	10%	$37	$0.6	$0.2	$1.1
2006	13%	$46	$0.9	$0.2	$1.4
2007	9%	$55	$0.7	$0.3	$1.7
2008	6%	$65	$0.6	$0.3	$1.9
				(in Billions)	
15% Cash Payout on Bogus Investment Returns per Year				$6	
Madoff Fees at 0.5% of AUM/Year				$2	
Redemption Payouts at 3% of AUM/Year				$11	
Cumulative Cash Payout				*$18*	

Note: This hypothetical account is based on several assumptions regarding yearly fund growth, cash payouts, and cash retained by Madoff. Actual cash distributions may have been significantly different.

Why the Music Stopped

Given the cash flows highlighted in Table 7-4, Madoff needed to raise just $2.5 to $3 billion of new capital per year to keep the plates of his $65 billion fraud spinning—not really that difficult, given the breadth of his marketing network and the spectacularly consistent returns he was reporting. The sand-in-the-gears scenario of any good fraud, of course, is the possibility that a large number of investors will ask for their money back en masse. Well, Bernie, welcome to the credit crisis of 2008. When a tsunami of redemptions hit the hedge fund industry, even the strongest performing funds became ATMs for investors who needed money and could not access cash from gated or suspended funds.

Unfortunately for Madoff, his fund became one of these ATMs. With 2008 drawing to a close, Madoff apparently received close to $7 billion of redemption requests. Unable to raise enough capital to satisfy the requests, he finally threw in the towel, ending a scheme that just might have outlived its creator but for the 100-year storm that rocked the industry and revealed one of the largest and longest running deceptions in history.

Let's assume the calculations in Table 7-4 are correct and $18 billion in cash was paid out through Ponzi "investment returns," redemptions, and other payments. A bankruptcy trustee will argue that at least a portion of these past gains and distributions were simply a fraudulent redistribution of other investors' capital. Consequently, investors could be asked to return any cash payments (principal redemption proceeds or capital returns) from as far back as three to six years. The trustee would pool those assets and redistribute the proceeds among all investors. This arrangement would be good for those left holding the bag at the end but bad for those smart enough or lucky enough to have gotten out before the collapse.

The first shot in what will likely be a bitter, multiyear battle among investors was fired in April 2009 when the Madoff trustee overseeing recovery of assets sued Vizcaya Partners, a British Virgin

Islands–based Madoff investor, seeking recovery of $150 million in funds that were withdrawn six weeks before the Madoff fraud was uncovered.

Failed Attempts at Detection

That such a thinly veiled fraud could exist on such an epic scale for nearly 20 years is one of the most mystifying aspects of the story. Madoff's success in evading detection probably owes much to the combination of lax industry oversight, failed regulatory reviews, and complacency on the part of investors who were entranced by the near perfection of the returns.

There was, however, one man, Harry Markopolos, who in November 2005 sent the SEC a 17-page letter entitled "The world's largest hedge fund is a fraud." He outlined no fewer than 29 red flags in the Madoff operation and raised many of the questions that the rest of world is now asking.

The SEC actually investigated Madoff in response to Markopolos's tip but found nothing improper. In fact, the SEC has reviewed Madoff's operation eight times over the past 16 years. These reviews, with the possible exception of the one Markopolos triggered, probably focused more on the firm's trading activities and its potential for "front running" client orders to generate internal trading profits than the potential for a $65 billion pyramid scheme. Whatever they thought, Madoff's Jolly Roger sailed on, past one regulatory review after another.

If there is a deeper lesson that emerges from the Madoff scandal, it may be that the best frauds are those that give investors everything they could possibly hope to achieve in a legitimate investment but never more than they might rationally expect to receive. In doing so, the fraud succeeds as victims soften their standards of diligence to reach for that perfection. In the end, the only defense is disciplined adherence to strong diligence standards.

The Bayou Fraud: A Mini Madoff

All the means of deceit found in Madoff's toolbox were also used in another high profile hedge fund fraud perpetrated by the Bayou Hedge Fund Group. Bayou was founded by Samuel Israel III in 1996 as a short-term, long-short equity, and commodity trading fund. It employed a strategy commonly known as "day trading," in which traders seek to exit most trades at the close of every trading day.

Israel was born to a prominent New Orleans family. His grandfather, the first Samuel Israel, founded a commodity trading company, ACLI International, which he built up into a powerhouse and sold to the Wall Street firm of Donaldson, Lufkin & Jenrette in 1981 for $44 million.[5] Like Madoff and many before him, Israel used his pedigree to affirm his stature as an established Wall Street player. After attending Tulane University for seven semesters, Israel dropped out and headed north to Wall Street to attempt to sustain his family's legacy. He worked for a number of street firms, including Omega Partners, a $4 billion hedge fund run by Leon Cooperman.

After his brief stint with Omega, Israel launched Bayou, marketing his experience as "head trader" for Omega from 1992 to 1996, where he claimed to have been "responsible for all equity and financial futures executions." Omega representatives later said that this characterization was false and described Israel as an "administrative employee" who executed trade orders over the much shorter tenure of 18 months.[6] In founding Bayou, Israel partnered with his friend Daniel Marino, who acted as both COO and CFO.

Despite the embellishments on Israel's resume, his incomplete education, and relative lack of asset management experience, he somehow launched the fund in early 1996 with a relatively modest amount of capital. Undoubtedly, this initial success owed more to his family's wealth, reputation, and connections than to Israel's personal acumen.

Unfortunately for his initial investors, Israel was, from the start, a lousy manager of capital. According to federal prosecutors, his investment strategies never successfully generated any legitimate positive returns. Instead, as the losses piled up, Israel and Marino turned to the grab bag of standard hedge fund deceptions and built up their own Ponzi scheme that ran for nine years.

At first, the scheme was relatively modest in scope, as the fund had only $16.5 million under management in 2000. Like Madoff, however, Israel ramped up his capital by reporting consistently positive, uncorrelated returns pulled from a magic hat of fictitious numbers. Not surprisingly, the returns drew the attention of many investors struggling in the uncertain market environment created by the collapse of the tech bubble, 9/11, and a deep recession.

As highlighted in Table 7-7, from 2000 to 2002, Bayou reported fictitious cumulative gains of more than 25% against a decline in the S&P 500 Index of more than 40%. Over the same period, the fund reported that AUM rocketed up from $16.5 million to $148.8 million as investors clamored for exposure to a fund that could somehow

Table 7-7 Bayou AUM and Annual Returns versus the S&P 500

	AUM ($MM)	Net Profit ($MM)	Bayou Annual Return	S&P 500
2000	$16.50	$2.00	12.1%	−9.1%
2001	$85.40	$4.20	4.9%	−11.9%
2002	$148.80	$12.90	8.7%	−22.1%
2003	$323.00	$43.20	13.4%	28.7%
2004	$410.60	$54.30	13.2%	10.9%
		Average	10.5%	

Source: *Commodity Futures Trading Commission v. Bayou Management LLC, et al.*

produce such extraordinary gains in the midst of such a miserable market environment. As the bogus positive returns continued into 2003 and 2004, so did the inflow of capital: total AUM, pumped up by FOFs, consultants, and high net worth individuals, topped $400 million.

To ensure that curious, duly diligent minds did not spoil the fun, Israel took another page from Madoff's playbook, blocking almost all service provider or counterparty access to the fund's details. The first step was to fully self-administrate. Bayou priced its own securities, generated its own monthly financial statements for investors, and calculated its own fees. Sound familiar? Next, Marino set up a sham accounting firm, Richmond-Fairfield Associates, which issued fake year-end audits attesting to the bogus positive investment returns. With strikingly little sophistication, Marino equipped Richmond-Fairfield with the necessary, if thin, façade of legitimacy. His ruse appears to have included only leased office space, a separate telephone number, a Web site, and an e-mail address. When Bayou investors made inquiries, Marino often handled the calls himself, usually under an assumed name, such as "Mathew Richmond." Like a bad detective show, "gotcha" clues were everywhere. Israel was listed as the registrant of the Richmond-Fairfield Web site, Richmond-Fairfield.com, and the Web site's domain registry was recorded as bayoufund@aol.com.[7]

As a final barrier to inquiring eyes, Israel created a broker-dealer that would custody and execute trades on behalf of Bayou's hedge funds. As with Madoff, this allowed Israel and his partners to conceal the absence of physical positions and Bayou's money-losing trading activity while continuing to bilk investors out of trading fees.

With nearly all independent access to fund information blocked, investors had two choices: overlook grossly inadequate transparency and process controls in exchange for exceptionally attractive historical returns, or maintain discipline and potentially miss out on the "perfect" return profile down the road. Unfortunately, most investors behind Bayou's $450 million chose door number one.

Interestingly, the one legitimate counterparty that had some insight into the firm's activities was a unit of Goldman Sachs, which acted as the firm's prime broker for a period of time.[8] Unfortunately, Goldman provided prime brokerage services on only a portion of the firm's portfolio and therefore never had access to the entire picture.

Throughout the incredible nine years that this deception flew beneath the radar, Israel charged investors a 20% performance fee for the fictitious returns the fund reported (see Table 7-8) and paid himself and his partners more than $20 million in the final years of the fraud.

Table 7-8 Bayou "Performance Fees"

	Bayou "Performance Fees"
2000	$399,130
2001	$834,555
2002	$2,586,635
2003	$8,631,935
2004	$10,861,578

Source: Commodity Futures Trading Commission v. Bayou Management LLC, et al.

Like Madoff, but on a slightly less ambitious scale, Israel and Marino ensconced themselves in a lifestyle befitting successful Ponzi men. According to the *New York Times*, Israel rented a 10-bedroom stone mansion, originally built for ketchup mogul H. J. Heinz, for $32,000 a month. Not to be left out, Marino began cruising the streets in a new Bentley and moved up from a modest Staten Island home to a multimillion-dollar estate in Westport, Connecticut.

The End of the Road

After years of unsuccessful attempts to create legitimate trading gains, Israel's behavior became increasingly erratic. In early 2003, he closed the original Bayou Fund and inexplicably created four successor funds: the Bayou Accredited Fund LLC, the Bayou Affiliates Fund LLC, the Bayou No Leverage Fund LLC, and the Bayou Superfund LLC. With little apparent success in generating a profit in any of these successor funds, Israel ceased all trading activity in the spring of 2004. After at least six years without a legitimate trading profit, any hope of "earning" his way back to legitimacy through day trading activities had fizzled. From this point until late 2005, when the scheme finally unraveled, Israel and Marino must have felt the walls closing in around them. In desperation, they pursued a number of questionable private investments that promised returns large enough to cover up the fraud and keep them out of jail. Ironically, the largest of these investments involved a bizarre international scheme in which Israel and Marino were themselves swindled. Fortunately for Bayou investors, the number of wire transfers required to execute the $150 million investment attracted the attention of the authorities and much of this money was later recovered.[9]

Israel's scheme fell apart in August 2005 when Silver Creek Capital Management, a large FOF, sought to withdraw $53 million from Bayou. After years of trading losses and theft of capital, Bayou was in no position to meet this redemption request. When a principal from Silver Creek arrived at Bayou's office for a meeting on August 16, he found a note on Marino's desk that began "My name is Dan Marino and this is a combined confession and suicide letter . . . for the past seven years, I have committed a fraud of great magnitude."[10]

Marino didn't actually kill himself. Instead, he and Israel confessed and pleaded guilty in 2005 to several counts of conspiracy and investment advisory fraud. Marino is currently serving 20 years in federal prison.

Israel, for his part, is currently serving a 30-year sentence. In a final twist, just days before his long vacation at federal expense was to begin, Israel also apparently contemplated killing himself, writing "suicide is painless" on the windshield of his ditched SUV. He spent several months on the lam in a motor home before finally surrendering to authorities.

Clawback

In 2007, a bankruptcy court ruled that all assets that had been redeemed from Bayou funds in the two years preceding the bankruptcy filing had to be turned over to a bankruptcy trustee. The trustee then repooled these with other recovered assets and redistributed all recovered capital to investors on a pro rata basis. Like the Hotel California, Ponzi schemes are easy to check into but very difficult to leave.

Perhaps the most shocking aspect of the Bayou case is how obvious it seems in hindsight. As with the Madoff fraud, it is particularly surprising that investors with large due diligence staffs did not heed the many warning signs: self-administration, the use of an obscure auditor, and an internal broker-dealer.

The DNA of Fraud

Bayou and Madoff, for all the misery they visited on the hedge fund industry, might still deliver a silver lining. Both scandals were so massive, in terms of scale and longevity, that taken together they provide a comprehensive manual for how to spot fraud in the hedge fund industry.

Both funds were self-administrated, both self-custodied their positions, both utilized internal trading operations, and both steered clear of nationally recognized auditing firms. As classic Ponzi schemes, both required new cash to support the bogus returns paid to existing investors and collapsed as soon as the weight of investor redemptions overwhelmed their ability to raise new capital. Finally, both conducted trading strategies that few if any other hedge funds in the market could employ successfully. If the industry can remove any of these risks from hedge fund investment portfolios, it will go a long way toward eliminating fraud.

A final word on this type of fraud: If a fund is managing several hundred million dollars of investor capital and generating millions of dollars in annual management fees, it can afford to have a top fund administrator, such as Citco Fund Services or State Street; a leading auditor, such as PricewaterhouseCoopers, Deloitte & Touche, KPMG, Ernst & Young, or Grant Thornton; and strong prime brokerage or lending relationships at firms such as Goldman Sachs, Morgan Stanley, Citigroup, Bank of America, UBS, etc. If a big fund is sailing along without such affiliations, an investor's decision should be easy: pass, no matter what type of returns the fund has been posting.

Fraud 2.0

Once investors have satisfied themselves that the basic elements of strong fund governance are in place, they must also consider the ways a fraud can succeed despite the engagement of top service providers and counterparties. Probably the most fertile ground for this more elusive type of fraud is in investment activity that is not easily processed by the standard systems of a hedge fund administrator or auditor. Investments that fall into this category include any number of private debt or equity securities, unique or structurally complex securities, and other privately designed derivative instruments.

Without an exchange listing or another active market for these investments, hedge fund administrators can find it difficult to establish a legitimate valuation level for the portfolio. Instead, the administrator will look to either a third party or the managers themselves to provide the valuation. If a fund has a high concentration of illiquid, highly structured, or private investments and is utilizing its own models and model inputs to value these securities, the likelihood of inconsistent valuations or fraud can increase significantly.

Why? Because hedge fund compensation and self-valuation are a natural breeding ground for conflict. Hedge funds are, at their core, entrepreneurial businesses in which small groups of individuals stand to reap enormous personal gains. Even if a "Chinese wall" separates the portfolio manager from the individual responsible for valuing his portfolio of illiquid securities, the potential for improper influence is high. Funds that manage large portfolios of illiquid or hard to value securities should always utilize an independent third party to verify their valuations. If they don't, proceed with caution.

A "Softer" Type of Fraud

Surveillance of "hard fraud," in which theft or misappropriation of capital is involved (as was the case with Madoff and Bayou), has always been a priority of both regulators and investors. Other "soft" forms of fraud, such as misleading investor communications, have historically tended to receive less attention from both groups.

The 2007–2008 market crisis changed that relative perception. The collapse of several large hedge funds during this period highlighted the potential for inconsistent, inaccurate, and potentially fraudulent communication at critical junctures in the life of a hedge fund. In particular, the recent indictments of two Bear

Stearns hedge fund managers, on charges of providing investors with misleading information just prior to the collapse and 100% investor loss in two of their hedge funds, demonstrate the potential economic impact involved. In many cases, including Bear Stearns, allegations of communication fraud occur in funds with accurate accounting, proper securities valuation, and otherwise operationally "clean" businesses. Even for these well-managed funds, times of severe stress can create particular vulnerability to communication fraud. During these periods, sharply declining performance, investor redemption requests, and debt covenant breaches can lead to precarious moments in which full and timely disclosure of negative information will also negatively impact capital stability, fund performance, future fee income, and ultimately the survival of the business itself.

The Alleged Bear Fraud

Chapter 1 examined the factors that led to the failure of the Bear funds in July 2007. Roughly a year later, in June 2008, Ralph Cioffi and Matthew Tannin were indicted on charges of securities fraud for allegedly providing investors with inaccurate and misleading information in the months leading up to the funds' collapse.

As you will recall from our earlier discussion, Cioffi was the founder and senior portfolio manager of the Bear Stearns High-Grade Structured Credit Strategies Master Fund (the "High-Grade Fund") and the High-Grade Structured Credit Strategies Enhanced Leverage Master Fund (the "Enhanced Fund"). Matthew Tannin was a portfolio manager who reported to Cioffi. The case against Cioffi and Tannin is based largely on the following allegations: In the months prior to the collapse, both were aware that the funds were in grave condition and at risk of failure. Rather than disclosing the true condition of the vehicles to investors and lenders, they misrepresented or omitted material facts in the hope that the funds would turn around and their incomes and reputations would remain intact.[11] Both Cioffi and Tannin have pleaded not guilty to these charges and are awaiting trial.

The Case against Ralph Cioffi and Matthew Tannin

To understand the basis for the case against Cioffi and Tannin, it is helpful to quickly review the background of the funds. In the fall of 2004, the High-Grade Fund was launched with an investment strategy targeted toward (seemingly) low-risk, high-grade debt securities, primarily AAA- and AA-rated tranches of collateralized debt obligations (CDOs). A CDO is a security with a pool of other debt instruments backing up its payment of interest and principal, typically mortgages or other corporate debt securities. The High-Grade Fund focused on investments in CDOs that were primarily backed by subprime (lower credit quality) residential mortgages. In order to achieve returns of 10% to 12%, net of fees, on relatively low-yielding CDO investments, the High-Grade Fund sought to utilize a significant amount of short-term leverage.

In the indictment, Cioffi and Tannin are said to have positioned the fund as a safe and steady investment, not designed to "hit home runs," and only slightly riskier than a money market fund. Before the credit crisis, this set of expectations for a leveraged investment in AA- and AAA-rated securities wasn't inconsistent with other funds pursuing similar strategies. In fact, for the first few years, returns for the High-Grade Fund generally met these expectations.

By 2006, however, the fund's performance had started to erode, and investor redemptions began to grow. According to the indictment, in August 2006, Cioffi sought to address both of these issues by launching a new fund, the Enhanced Leverage Fund. This fund would also invest primarily in subprime CDOs but—theoretically—would generate even higher returns with limited additional risk through a combination of higher leverage and greater focus on more highly rated (AAA) securities.

At this time, both Cioffi and Tannin allegedly told investors that they were moving their own personal funds from the High-Grade Fund to the Enhanced Fund. At the end of the marketing period for the Enhanced Fund, Cioffi and his partners succeeded in raising approximately $600 million in investor capital on top of the roughly $1.5 billion that remained invested in the High-Grade Fund.

Unfortunately, the glow of such a successful launch faded quickly. By February 2007, the Enhanced Fund reported a loss of −0.08%—the first loss that either fund had ever recorded.

It is about this time that the fraud allegations against Cioffi and Tannin begin to take shape. As the spring of 2007 unfolded and market conditions deteriorated, both are said to have expressed concern about the funds to one another and other colleagues. In a March 2007 meeting, the indictment alleges that Cioffi told Tannin that "the worry for me is that subprime losses will be far worse than anything people have modeled. . . ." A few days later in an e-mail to a colleague, Cioffi allegedly confessed, "I'm fearful of these markets. Matt [Tannin] said it's either a meltdown or the greatest buying opportunity ever. I'm leaning toward the former. As we discussed, it may not be a meltdown for the general economy but in our world it will be." By late March, Cioffi was said to have told a colleague that he was "sick to his stomach" over the fund's performance.[12]

As these conversations were taking place, another problem was beginning to brew: liquidity. Internal Bear Stearns Asset Management (BSAM) reports showed that the High-Grade Fund was in a precarious liquidity position. The indictment quotes Cioffi as saying, "[W]e do need to take positions down in the [High-Grade Fund]. We are getting loads of margin calls."[13]

In an effort to solve the liquidity problem, the indictment alleges that Cioffi and Tannin deliberately continued their aggressive marketing of the funds to investors while knowing that the outlook for the funds was becoming increasingly bleak. To support this claim, it cites several quotes or other communications with investors: Cioffi is said to have told a Bear Stearns broker with more than 40 clients in the fund that the current situation was "an awesome opportunity." Tannin was allegedly upbeat as well, telling an investor, "[W]e are seeing opportunities now and are excited about what is possible. I am adding capital to the fund. If you guys are in a position to do the same, I think this is a good opportunity." Highlighting the conflict they faced, Tannin was said to have e-mailed a colleague with the message, "[B]elieve it or not—I've been able to convince people to add more money."

Despite these statements, the indictment alleges that Tannin didn't invest additional personal capital in either fund, and Cioffi actually transferred $2 million of his approximately $6 million investment in the Enhanced Fund to another Bear fund.

As March 2007 drew to a close, the performance numbers for the funds began to deteriorate significantly. The High-Grade Fund reported a return of −3.71%, the Enhanced Fund −5.41%. As the funds performance declined, redemption requests naturally grew. In early April, one of the fund's three largest investors told BSAM that it wished to redeem its entire $57 million investment.[14]

The indictment goes on to allege that an internal "CDO report" was produced in April 2007, which showed that the value of the CDOs held by the fund was significantly lower than had previously been determined.[15] With the performance of the Enhanced Fund in danger of approaching −20% for the month, Tannin is said to have recommended to Cioffi that they either close the funds or significantly change their investment strategy. Tannin is quoted as saying that "the subprime market looks pretty damn ugly. . . . If we believe the [CDO report] is *anywhere close* to accurate I think we should close the funds now. The reason for this is if the [CDO report] is correct then the entire subprime market is toast. . . . If AAA bonds are systematically downgraded then there is simply no way for us to make money—ever." He went on to say that "caution would lead us to conclude that the report is right—and we are in bad bad shape." Despite these apparent grim predictions, Cioffi and Tannin allegedly agreed keep the funds' problems to themselves.[16]

An investor conference call on April 25 provided some of the most potent ammunition for the case against Cioffi and Tannin. In contrast to the bleak outlook he'd apparently been articulating privately, Tannin allegedly told investors,

> So, from a structural point of view, from an asset point of view, from a surveillance point of view, we're very comfortable with exactly

where we are. . . . The structure of the fund has performed exactly the way it was designed to perform. . . . It is really a matter of whether one believes that careful credit analysis makes a difference, or whether you think that this is just one big disaster. And there is no basis for thinking this is one big disaster.

Cioffi was also said to have addressed what is always a popular topic for a hedge fund in times of stress—redemptions: "I believe we only have a couple of million of redemptions for the June 30 date," he stated. Tannin is said to have echoed similar remarks about low redemptions. Despite Cioffi's and Tannin's claims, the fund had, according to the indictment, received redemption requests totaling at least $60 million. Cioffi also allegedly failed to mention that he himself had apparently redeemed money from the Enhanced Fund less than a month earlier.[17]

As the losses and margin calls mounted, investors were finally notified that all redemptions were suspended. A few days later, they were informed that the final April performance was −5.09% and −18.97% for the High-Grade and Enhanced Funds, respectively. This was just the beginning of a downward spiral that ended in a total, 100% wipeout of investment value for both funds.

The indictment raises two important questions. First, did Cioffi and Tannin properly communicate key facts about the funds' situation to investors regarding redemptions, officer investment, margin calls, etc.? Second, did the two see the decline in subprime CDO debt as a deep value buying opportunity or did they somehow know that the market for these securities would continue to worsen dramatically? The first question, largely one of facts and circumstance, should be fairly straightforward for the courts to address. The second question, however, seems to involve an element of market prophecy. If Cioffi and Tannin knew the market for their investments would worsen, one might ask, why they didn't simply short sell more subprime ABX contracts (hedges) and attempt to save the performance of the funds?

Regardless of the lawsuit's outcome, this case highlights the tension that exists between managers and investor capital. Investor equity capital is the lifeblood of the fund, the foundation of its investment portfolio, and the fee source that richly compensates management. Investors, by definition, are entitled to full and fair disclosure of important information so they can make informed investment decisions. Fund managers, on the other hand, must provide this information and, at the same time, manage the resulting capital instability (debt and equity) that can arise from any negative information. Furthermore, they must do so in a way that maximizes value for all investors (both those seeking redemption and those wishing to stay), regardless of the impact on the fund's future size or fee income. For some fund managers, that's not always an easy needle to thread.

Fortunately for investors and managers, the definition of information fraud that will emerge following the Bear case will, in all likelihood, create clearer guidelines for the industry and greatly reduce the potential for communication fraud in the future. Perhaps the final defense against any kind of investment fraud is sound portfolio management. If you maintain a well-diversified portfolio of hedge fund investments, any loss you sustain as a result of fraud will feel more like a surface wound than a lost body part.

Conclusion

THE ROAD TO
REDEMPTION

Like many other tales of runaway excess that end in a humbling return to reality, this story also includes a revival. The lost capital, collapsed funds, fraud, and other misfortunes cataloged in this book have produced outcomes so egregious that many investors will demand and receive substantial improvements to the hedge fund vehicles that remain. These changes will produce funds that provide more stable capital structures, performance fees that better align investor objectives with manager incentives, and greater transparency—all of which will promote better risk management and more sustainable growth long term.

Furthermore, the catastrophic losses suffered by many hedge funds have, ironically, set the stage for substantially better future returns for the industry. The deleveraging and forced asset sales wrought by the credit crisis have left many asset classes at historically low valuation levels. Surviving funds have the opportunity to offer better risk-adjusted returns now that there are fewer, less leveraged funds competing for the assets.

The disappearance of limitless leverage will also help to eliminate incidences of "artificial" alpha arising from the practice of magnifying small mundane spreads with high leverage, further separating the imposters from truly talented generators of excess returns.

Regulators will also have a voice. Pushed over the edge by the Madoff fraud, hedge fund collapses, and a perceived hedge fund role in the credit crisis, regulators are seeking and will inevitably gain significantly more oversight of the industry.

In total, these changes will serve to accelerate the transformation of the industry from thousands of small operators to a handful of large, $50 to $100 billion financial institutions. The increased cost of regulation, operations, and financing—along with the continuing demand for stable, institutional quality firms—will push thousands of smaller funds out of business. For most investors, these will be welcome changes.

The Future of Fees

Although many investors have called for industrywide lower fees, it is not clear that the events of 2008 and 2009 have demonstrated that all managers were overpaid at 2% and 20%. As in any other industry, exceptional producers will always be able to command premium fees. The size of investment should also be a factor. An investor who puts up $1 million should probably pay more, percentage-wise, than one who invests $500 million. Either way, these are mainly supply-and-demand questions that should be hashed out on a fund-by-fund basis.

Fee structures and the incentives they produce are a different matter. Although they may vary among different strategies or asset classes, they should always seek to balance and align manager and investor incentives.

Funds that pursue strategies with highly liquid underlying assets, such as many long-short equity funds, global macro, or commodity managers, should have different fee structures than funds that manage less liquid assets. Fee clawback features, for example, are arguably less useful for managers of liquid, easily tradable assets. These funds have the flexibility to realize profits whenever capital is redeemed at current market levels. As a result, performance in any one period is generally representative of realized returns for that period. In these cases it may be more important to achieve alignment through increased ownership in the fund.

Investors should also seek to invest with managers who have a substantial amount of their own net worth in their funds. Beyond this initial screen, a provision requiring managers to further invest 50% to 75% of all annual performance fees in the fund for a period of three years would create additional ownership by fund managers and better align incentives.

For managers investing in longer-dated and possibly less liquid assets, a mechanism to hold back or claw back performance fees is more important. In these cases, funds should be subject to a clawback on performance fees over a period of time that matches the duration of the underling assets in a stressed environment. For many credit managers, this is probably at least two to three years. Because it is hard to claw back money already paid to individuals, performance fees would need to be escrowed and paid out to the manager over time. If performance suffers in the out years, those performance fees would be returned to investors. This type of structure would help to eliminate the scenario discussed in

Chapter 1, in which an investor pays performance fees on returns that often disappear upon liquidation of the underlying assets.

In general, hedge fund fees should be structured to create a more equal ownership of both the upside and the downside in the fund. When necessary, performance fees should be paid over a period that best approximates the duration of the underlying assets.

Together, these changes will encourage greater manager downside ownership and restrict performance fee payment to performance realization. Both of these objectives are key to aligning the interests of managers and investors and to creating more sustainable long-term value for both.

Transparency

If there was any argument against greater transparency in hedge funds, Bernie Madoff ended it. Even beyond the Madoff fraud, the credit crisis highlighted that hedge fund leverage was, in many cases, excessively high, dangerously short term, and unwisely used to support illiquid assets. For many investors, the true risk of this leverage and its covenants was not well disclosed or understood. To get a clearer picture of all of the risks inherent in a hedge fund, investors must have access to significantly more transparency on both the asset and liability side of the balance sheet. Some of the most important items include:

Asset Level Transparency
- Total long and short exposure by strategy, geography, sector, and security type

- Monthly return attribution by strategy, geography, sector, and security type

- 10 to 20 largest long and short positions and their current marks
- Description and notional amount of derivatives utilized
- Assessment of asset liquidity in portfolio by security
- Disclosure of pricing source for assets—market, model, etc.
- Weekly and monthly return estimates
- AUM, monthly
- Leverage, gross and by strategy

Equity Capital Transparency
- Investor base information: investor type, concentration by top holders, and geography
- Proportion of capital subject to lockup listed by lockup duration
- "Side letters" or other deals offering special terms to select investors

Debt Capital Transparency
- Amount and source of debt utilized
- Terms of each source of debt—cost, duration, collateral, recourse/nonrecourse
- Key covenants—NAV triggers, margin requirements, key man provisions, etc.

Armed with this information, an investor will be in a much better position to understand a fund's leverage levels, debt and equity stability, asset liquidity, security pricing accuracy, and other important data points. Viewed in aggregate, this data will provide a much clearer picture of risk at a hedge fund. Without it, an investor is basically flying blind, and when periods of stress hit, blind capital is far more likely to exit than informed capital. As a result, transparency can actually contribute to greater equity capital stability.

A general standard for acceptable transparency is a must for the industry. It is a necessary component of identifying poor managers of risk and facilitating the efficient flow of capital to more capable funds. It will also help to reduce fraud, improve capital stability, and, ultimately, restore investor trust. In short, it is critical to the future success of the industry.

Leverage and Capital Stability

Leverage was a catalyst for both the explosive growth and downfall of the hedge fund industry. It made imposters look smart, it was addictive, and the withdrawal symptoms were violent. However, funds that employ leverage are not always courting disaster. The risk it introduces is a function of three factors: the amount of leverage employed, the stability of the fund's equity capital, and the duration and liquidity of the assets being leveraged relative to the term of the debt.

At one end of the risk spectrum are funds that seek prudent amplification of returns through modest shorter-term leverage on highly liquid, well-hedged assets. At the other end is the toxicity of excessive short-term leverage and three-month equity capital supporting potentially illiquid long-term assets. Both situations involve debt; one is advisable and prudent, the other is frequently deadly.

Given these facts, how will the use of leverage evolve? First, and maybe most obviously, hedge funds will use significantly less leverage in the future. Banks have little interest in providing leverage at levels seen before the crisis, and investors, by demanding greater transparency in the funds they own, will move capital away from those that use leverage recklessly.

These changes solve part of the leverage problem, but they don't address the core issues of asset-liability duration mismatch and equity capital instability. Any effective solution to these problems must begin with greater equity capital stability. Currently, most funds allow redemptions to occur at the end of each calendar quarter but limit the total amount of capital that may be withdrawn from the fund through a gate mechanism. This methodology is reasonably effective for managers of liquid assets; most of these funds can meet redemptions efficiently by selling assets and returning capital within the redemption notice period. Managers of less liquid assets, however, face a much more daunting process loaded with negative incentives. Investors rightfully fear being the last to exit a fund that is being forced to sell its best assets first and least desirable assets last. This fear often results in a run on the bank that can be damaging to all investors.

For managers of less liquid assets, the current lockup mechanisms will have to change. In funds that hold multiyear duration assets prone to diminished liquidity in times of stress, investors should require at least a one-year rolling lockup (described below). If managers are unwilling to provide it, it simply means that the assets targeted by the strategy are not cheap enough to warrant an investment of that length. If investors withhold their capital from funds pursuing long-dated or illiquid assets long enough, the returns will rise to a level that draws longer-term capital back.

Rolling Lockups

Hedge fund capital stability can be further enhanced by implementing longer-term, one- or two-year lockups on a "rolling basis." As the term suggests, after investors complete the initial one-year lockup, they must choose either to roll their lockups forward for another year or redeem. This would replace the standard provision that requires a one-year lockup but allows quarterly liquidity thereafter.

A rolling lockup accomplishes two important goals. First, for managers of longer-dated assets, it does a significantly better job of matching investor capital to the underlying assets. Second, because investors enter funds at different times, it naturally staggers any potential redemptions throughout the year and reduces the pressure to sell at any one time.

Investor Level Gates

A rolling lockup can be further refined by utilizing "investor level gate" features in addition to fund level gates. Unlike standard fund level gates, which restrict withdrawals to a certain percentage of the overall fund, an investor level gate restricts investors from withdrawing more than a specified amount of *their* capital. If implemented with a rolling one-year lockup, this feature would allow redeeming investors to access up to 50% of their capital at the end of their lockup. The remainder would be available in the quarter or quarters that followed.

By staggering potential redemptions across quarters through rolling lockups and capping investor withdrawals through both fund and investor level gates, a manager of longer-dated assets can smooth the outflow of capital and improve the stability of the fund.

With these changes, equity capital stability can improve dramatically within a fund. "Run on the bank" incentives, NAV trigger violations, and forced asset sales can all be reduced. For FOFs and other short-term investors who may find these terms onerous, long-short equity, global macro, and other more liquid strategies will always be available.

For many leveraged managers of longer-dated assets, however, these measures address only part of the capital instability problem. For most of these funds, leverage is still essentially available only on a one-day to three-month rolling basis, and banks seem unlikely to commit to longer-term debt any time soon. As a result, investors should move capital away from managers that use high leverage (two to three times the fund's AUM or more) against illiquid assets. Those who use more prudent levels of leverage should keep greater cash balances on hand to mitigate the negative pressure of an abrupt loss of their financing.

Style Drift

Chapter 5, "The Hedge Fund Peter Principle," addressed the danger of style drift. For investors, this problem is rooted in the contractual discretion explicitly provided to many managers that allows them to pursue investments across a nearly unlimited scope of asset classes without shareholder notice or approval. This arrangement grew out of a desire to allow managers broad access to the best opportunities. Unfortunately for many investors, 2008 proved that one manager's talents do not apply to all strategies and asset classes. To put it colloquially, you probably don't want a brain surgeon performing your open-heart surgery, even if they're both brilliant physicians.

As investor capital returns to hedge funds over time, a more focused description of investment activities in a fund's offering memorandum would be helpful to investors. It wouldn't necessarily prevent the manager from capturing the next short subprime mortgage opportunity, but it would force him to set up a new fund with dedicated managers to capture it. Investors could then vote with their capital and decide whether to support this new opportunity or not. If longer-term lockups are going to be part of the new hedge fund landscape, then broad guidelines around strategic investment focus will also be very important.

Fraud: Sunlight Is the Best Disinfectant

Of the many hedge fund flaws that have been revealed, it's likely that none had as devastating an effect on investor trust as the perpetration of massive frauds. Without reliable methods of preventing future scams, that trust will be hard to restore.

Fortunately, Madoff and Bayou have effectively provided a detailed fraud road map that both reveals the mechanics of the scams and points to the tools for preventing them in the future. Both funds were self-administrated, self-custodied their positions, and were reliant on internal trading operations. Both inexplicably avoided established or nationally recognized auditing firms. They ostensibly conducted trading strategies that few if any other hedge funds in the market could successfully replicate but offered little or no transparency to support their apparent success. Finally, both were structured as Ponzi schemes and required new cash to support the bogus returns paid to existing investors, and both collapsed only when the weight of investor redemptions overwhelmed their ability to raise that new capital. Address each of these gaping governance holes, and future frauds will be significantly harder to conceal.

Avoiding Future Frauds

- Fund transparency (as outlined above)
- Fund administration conducted only by an independent third party
- Security custody conducted only by an independent third party
- Audits performed by a nationally recognized audit firm
- Established outside trading partners
- Independent boards of directors, where applicable

These measures on their own are no diligence panacea, however strictly they are observed, but they do provide a framework for improvements to the industry's current best practices. Of course, the challenge will be to monitor the extent to which funds implement these improvements.

The Power of Capital

Fortunately for hedge fund investors, the pain of 2008 has a positive side: those with capital to invest have never enjoyed more leverage over hedge fund managers than they do today. Given this opportunity, it is incumbent upon them to use the power of their capital to effect rational improvements that will create better and more sustainable risk-adjusted returns within the industry.

Some investors are already moving in this direction. Letters have surfaced from influential institutional investors such as CalPERS (the California Pension Retirement System) and URS (the Utah Retirement System) advocating a number of these changes. If this is a beginning, it appears that investors face a much brighter future in the hedge fund industry. The same may hold true for hedge fund managers who are willing to evolve and adapt. For those who do, growth will return, capital will be more stable, and returns will improve. Along the way, that pickled shark might have to be downsized to a piranha, but hey, a piranha has plenty of teeth too.

ENDNOTES

Introduction

1. Hedge Fund Research, Inc.
2. AIMA's Roadmap to Hedge Funds, November 2008.

Chapter 1

1. Catherine Boyle, "Job Cuts at Meriwether Hedge Fund," Times Online, April 28, 2008, http://business.timesonline.co .uk/tol/business/industry_sectors/banking_and_finance/ article3835160.ece.
2. Gwen Robinson, "Peloton Founder Tries Again," ft.com, January 12, 2009, http://ftalphaville.ft.com.

Chapter 2

1. *Wall Street Journal*, October 16, 2008.
2. Hedge Fund Alert, October 15, 2008.
3. Tom Cahill, "Lehman Hedge-Fund Clients Left Cold as Asset Frozen," Bloomberg, October 1, 2008.
4. Jenny Strasburg and Katherine Burton, "Sowood Funds Lose More Than 50% as Debt Markets Fall," Bloomberg, July 31, 2007.
5. Gregory Zuckerman and Craig Karmin, "Sowood's Short, Hot Summer," *Wall Street Journal*, October 27, 2007.

6. Steven Syre, "Sowood Founder Apologizes," *The Boston Globe*, August 4, 2007.
7. Zuckerman and Karmin, "Sowood's Short, Hot Summer."
8. Ibid.
9. Ibid.
10. Yalman Onaran and Jody Shenn, "Cioffi's Hero-to-Villain Hedge Funds Masked Bear Peril in CDOs," Bloomberg, July 3, 2007.
11. Matthew Goldstein and David Henry, "Bear Stearns' Bad Bet," *BusinessWeek*, October 11, 2007.
12. United States of America Indictment against Ralph Cioffi and Matthew Tannin 6/19/2008.
13. Kate Kelly and Serena Ng, "Lifeline, Bear Stearns Bails Out Fund with Big Loan," *Wall Street Journal*, June 23, 2007.
14. Ibid.
15. United States of America Indictment against Ralph Cioffi and Matthew Tannin, June 19, 2008.
16. Kelly and Ng, "Lifeline, Bear Stearns Bails Out Fund with Big Loan."
17. United States of America Indictment against Ralph Cioffi and Matthew Tannin, June 19, 2008.
18. Kelly and Ng, "Lifeline, Bear Stearns Bails Out Fund with Big Loan."
19. Ibid.
20. Ibid.

Chapter 3

1. Andreas Cremer, "Volkswagen Stock Surges as Porsche Says It Aims for 75% Stake," Bloomberg, October 27, 2008.

Chapter 4

1. Louis Story, "Citadel Chief Denies Rumors of Trouble," *New York Times*, October 24, 2008.
2. Transcript of Citadel Conference Call, October 24, 2008.
3. Riva D. Atlas, "Hedge Funds, Rumors, and Sell-Off," *New York Times*, May 12, 2005.
4. Speech by SEC Chairman: Remarks Before the Foundation Financial Officers Group Spring Meeting by SEC Chairman William H. Donaldson, May 12, 2005, http://www.sec.gov/news/speech/spch051205whd.htm.

Chapter 5

1. *Excessive Speculation in the Natural Gas Market*, United States Senate Permanent Subcommittee on Investigations, June 25, 2007, http://hsgac.senate.gov/public/index.cfm?FuseAction=Subcommittees.Investigations.
2. Landon Thomas Jr., "Hedge Fund Turmoil: Effects on a High Flying Founder; Billions in Losses Dim a Star Manager's Glow," *New York Times*, September 20, 2006.
3. *Excessive Speculation in the Natural Gas Market*.
4. Ibid.
5. Ibid.
6. Ibid.
7. U.S. Commodity Futures Trading Commission Complaint against Amaranth Advisors LLC, Brian Hunter et al., United States District Court Southern District of New York, July 25, 2007.
8. Ann Davis, Gregory Zuckerman, and Henny Sender, "Hedge-Fund Hardball: How Amaranth Was Devoured by Its Banker, MorganChase," *Wall Street Journal*, January 30, 2007.

9. Thomas Watson, "Market Speculation: The Trials of Brian Hunter," *Canadian Business*, February 14, 2008.

10. *Excessive Speculation in the Natural Gas Market.*

11. Ibid.

12. Ibid.

13. Katherine Burton and Jenny Strasburg, "Amaranth's $6.6 Billion Slide Began with Trader's Bid to Quit," Bloomberg, December 6, 2006.

14. *Excessive Speculation in the Natural Gas Market.*

15. Ibid.

16. Ibid.

17. Ibid.

18. Ibid.

19. Ibid.

20. Ibid.

21. Ibid.

22. Ibid.

23. Ann Davis, "Amaranth Fund Sues J.P. Morgan Over Its Collapse," *Wall Street Journal*, November, 15, 2007.

Chapter 6

1. AIMA's Roadmap to Hedge Funds, November 2008.

2. Steel Partner's letter to investors, December 31, 2008.

3. Katherine Burton, "Steel Partners Seeks to Convert Biggest Fund to Public Company," Bloomberg, January 12, 2009.

4. *Bank of America, N.A. as Master Trustee of ACF Master Trust v. Steel Partners II LTD, et al.*, filed in the court of chancery for the State of Delaware, January 13, 2009.

5. Joseph A. Giannone, "Steel Partners Forges Ahead with Fund Conversion," Reuters, May 22, 2009.

6. Jenny Anderson, "Troubled Firm to Close 2 Funds Worth $4 Billion," *New York Times*, February 23, 2008.

7. Pipewire, "D.B. Zwirn to Liquidate Funds Worth $4B," February 25, 2008.

8. Henny Sender, "Meteoric Zwirn Falls Down to Earth," *Financial Times*, February 22, 2008.

9. Anderson, "Troubled Firm to Close 2 Funds Worth $4 Billion."

10. Jenny Strasburg, "Zwirn Shuts Hedge Funds After Clients Pull $2 Billion," Bloomberg, February 22, 2008.

11. Anderson, "Troubled Firm to Close 2 Funds Worth $4 Billion."

12. Henny Sender, "SEC Steps Up DB Zwirn Investigation," *Financial Times*, May 27, 2008.

13. Strasburg, "Zwirn Shuts Hedge Funds After Clients Pull $2 Billion."

14. Sender, "SEC Steps Up DB Zwirn Investigation."

Chapter 7

1. Fairfield Greenwich Group Fairfield Sentry Limited Investor presentation, October 2008.

2. *Inter-American Trust et al. v. Fairfield Greenwich Group et al.*, United States District Court Southern District of New York, January 12, 2009.

3. Philip Aldrick, "Madoff Victims Turn Spotlight on PwC Auditing Role," *Telegraph*, April 4, 2009.

4. Alyssa Abkowitz, "Madoff's Auditor . . . Doesn't Audit?" *Fortune*, December 19, 2008.

5. Thom Weidlich and David Gloven, "Bayou's Israel Gets 20-Year Term for Hedge Fund Fraud," Bloomberg, April 14, 2008.

6. Katherine Burton and RobUrban, "Bayou Fraud Exposes Tale of Lies, Drugs, Violence," Bloomberg, October 27, 2005.

7. Ibid.

8. Jenny Anderson, "Defrauded Fund Investors Sue Goldman," *New York Times,* July 18, 2008.

9. Burton and Urban, "Bayou Fraud Exposes Tale of Lies, Drugs, Violence."

10. Ibid.

11. *United States of America v. Ralph Cioffi and Matthew Tannin,* United States District Court Eastern District of New York, June 19, 2008.

12. Ibid.

13. Ibid.

14. Ibid.

15. Ibid.

16. Ibid.

17. Ibid.

INDEX

ABOUT THE AUTHOR

Trevor Ganshaw is a partner at a multi-strategy hedge fund in New York City. Ganshaw's articles have been published in the *Journal of Applied Corporate Finance*. He lives in Greenwich, Connecticut.